ELISABETTA ILLY

Aroma of the World

A JOURNEY INTO THE MYSTERIES
AND DELIGHTS OF COFFEE

WITH A PREFACE BY SANTO VERSACE

THE EXCLUSIVE RECIPES OF GIANFRANCO VISSANI

CONTRIBUTION BY ANDREA ILLY

WHITE STAR PUBLISHERS

Royalties will be donated to the Ernesto Illy Foundation – www.fondazionernestoilly.org

Original title: L'Aroma del Mondo
Italian Edition
Copyright © Ulrico Hoepli Editore S.p.A. 2010

English Edition:

WHITE STAR PUBLISHERS

White Star Publishers® is a registered trademark
property of De Agostini Libri S.p.A.

© 2012, 2014 De Agostini Libri S.p.A.
Via G. da Verrazano, 15
28100 Novara, Italy
www.whitestar.it - www.deagostini.it

Revised edition

Translation: Julian Comoy
Translation copyedited by: Katrina Read

ISBN 978-88-544-0924-8
1 2 3 4 5 6   18 17 16 15 14

Printed in China

Supervision: Roberto Morelli
Editorial coordination: Alessandra Zigliotto
Editorial coordinator for the English edition: Vanina Asquini
With contributions by Giacomo Celi, Alessio Colussi, Marino Petracco, Fabiana Pozzar, Luca Turello
In collaboration with the Università del caffè of illycaffè S.p.A.
www.unicaffè.com - www.illy.com

Picture research: Maurizio Cargnelli, Tullio Sega

Art direction: Maurizio Cargnelli
Graphic design: Andrej Vodopivec / Giotto Enterprise (Trieste)
Post production: Primož Birsa, Tullio Sega
Pagination: Giulio Dambrosi, Davide Martinelli
Jacket design: Maurizio Cargnelli

FOR YOU, NONNO ERNI

TABLE OF CONTENTS

PART TWO
THE WORLD IN A COFFEE BEAN

Preface

BY SANTO VERSACE

Coffee is my drink, the one I like best, the drink that punctuates my days and gives my life its rhythm. I drank my first coffee when I was a little boy. It was instant coffee from the States and my mother used it to make caffé au lait. I remember it as a happy moment in my day, when I would have breakfast with Gianni before going off to school: me to primary school, him still to nursery school. At the time I didn't realize how important this drink was; it was part of my daily routine and that was enough. It was only later that I got to enjoy real coffee. At home, like everywhere else, it was made with the moka percolator, and those first coffees sipped without being diluted with milk felt like a mark of emancipation. I was big enough to drink it like the grown ups, perhaps with a just little more sugar. So even then coffee marked a stage in my life. Today you would call it a "rite of passage", an initiation. But the real change, the step up, was a coffee drunk standing at the bar. I would sometimes go with my friends and school-mates to a bar to have an orangeade. The economic miracle was in full flow and for the first time we had a few coppers in our pockets and we loved the thought of drinking something at the bar just like grown-ups. The most daring, including myself, would order an espresso, not the usual fizzy drink or squash of some kind. It was the kind of daring deed that made us feel more grown up than the others, more confident, ready for fresh adventures.

The aroma rising from those scalding cups was the smell of emancipation. And, on top of that, it was good. I can still remember the slightly smoky atmosphere in those bars, where the sound of talking blended with the noise of people working at the bar, those afternoons spent sitting at a table with a coffee in front of me and a paper in my hands, trying to look cool. Little by little this ritual became an important part of my day, a chance to keep up with friends and make new ones.

But coffee was something else too: it kept me awake during my late nights when I was revising for my final school exams. I remember the short breaks I took to prepare another moka between a balance sheet and a mathematical formula as if it were yesterday. Coffee was my last resort between two and three in the morning, when the temptation to give in to sleep's sweet embrace seemed irresistible. But this dark, aromatic drink had an immediate effect and my friends and I were able to delve once again into the mysteries of algorithms and equations.

But I have other memories associated with coffee: I remember when I would sip it in the bar of the Genoa Cavalry Regiment with my fellow officers, after a tiring day spent on manoeuvres in the Carnia countryside. At the time we felt like characters in *The Tartar Steppe*, manning the forgotten Bastiano Fort frontier post. Our imagination was certainly working overtime... but that's the way it was. I have fond memories of those evenings spent in front of a steaming cup of coffee during what was an important experience for me.

So, coffee has always been and still is my favourite drink, and it was Gianni's too. During the frenzied work in the atelier to prepare our latest collection for a fashion show, coffee was an indispensable support. Sometimes we would overdo it and drink three or four one after another.

Over the years I've learnt to savour coffee. I used to just drink it without a moment's thought, but I've long since begun to appreciate the sequence of actions that make sipping a good coffee a ritual of extraordinary beauty. Everything contributes to the pleasure I take in it – the careful preparation, the quality of the service, the sensation I get from the feel of the cup in my hand and then the fragrance, the aromas, the enveloping flavour. From being a simple coffee drinker I've turned into an enthusiast, a devotee. I don't claim to be an expert, but I know what coffee I like, how I like it to be made and what I like to eat with it. And being Italian I'm lucky enough to be able to enjoy the best coffee in the world. It can't be an accident that in every country I've been to I've come across attempts to copy our espresso coffee, with varying degrees of success. There are some things that stand for a country: Italy is renowned throughout the world for the superb quality of its products, ranging from fashion to sports cars, food and precision engineering.

The *Made in Italy* label has established itself everywhere, just as Italian cooking and the Italian way of life have. One of these icons is precisely the espresso. The Italian way of making and drinking coffee will sweep all before it because it expresses a taste, a style, a capacity to appreciate the good things in life that everyone envies us and would like to copy.

That's why, among many other reasons, a good coffee is my favourite beverage.

DISCOVERING COFFEE

From plant to cup

THE EPIC STORY OF COFFEE, THROUGH HISTORY AND LEGEND

The story of coffee goes back generations and generations. Stretching back over one thousand years, taking in long series of events that have crossed the planet but are still swathed in mystery. It's all about the journey of a brown seed, full of secrets and curious facts.

Every time we drink a cup of coffee we are immersed in a world that has fascinated troubadours and scholars since time immemorial. The first legends regarding coffee are believed to have come out of the East four hundred years before the birth of Christ.

LEGENDS

Although European and Arab historians have gathered the echoes of mysterious stories that had their origins in Africa in the year five hundred, in the kingdom of the Queen of Sheba, the records that have come down to us suggest the plant was known for sure and coffee drunk in the first half of the fifteenth century. In the first treatise on coffee, *De Saluberrima potione* (1671), the monk Antonio Fausto Naironi tells the myth of the shepherd Kaldi, set in Ethiopia. One night Kaldi's sheep did not return from the fields and he went out to look for them. He found them the next day prancing around and full of beans,

Facing page: Sufi dancers in a 16th-century miniature. The 13th-century mystic al-Shadhili was among the first to use coffee beans to make a beverage. The *Shadhilites*, his followers and descendants, were Sufis and their ritual use of coffee (for example in the famous whirling Dervish dances) was frowned upon in more orthodox circles, as Islam expressly forbade the use of all "inebriating" substances. Sufi mystics were able to exploit coffee's stimulating properties to devote themselves to extremely long prayer sessions during which they would attain a state of religious ecstasy.

in this case literally, by a shiny green bush full of shiny red cherries. Intrigued by this strange behaviour, the shepherd tasted the berries and discovered how stimulating they were. So Kaldi embarked on a long journey to the monastery of Chehodet, in Yemen, at the southern tip of the Arabian peninsula, to tell the monks of his discovery. "It's the work of the devil!" opined a holy man, hurling the red cherries into the fire, where they promptly released a unique, mouth-watering aroma. The beans were quickly gathered up, ground and poured into a container full of hot water, making the first ever cup of coffee in the world. The monks found that this dark, bitter drink enabled them to go without sleep during the long nights spent praying. News about the effects of this delectable infusion spread from monastery to monastery and coffee began to be regarded as a veritable gift of God.

The legend concerning Mohammed is perhaps less familiar. One day the Prophet was struck by a sudden, irresistible drowsiness and the Archangel Gabriel came to his aid tendering a potion given to him by Allah himself. Mohammed drank it, felt his spirits pick up and went forth to continue his great exploits. Dark as the Holy Black Stone of the Kaaba, it is known as *qahwah* in the legend, a word that recalls the beverage's origins in a plant.

Coffee's long journey thus began in Africa, but it had a long way to go. It seems that in the thirteenth century slaves from the Sudan on their way to Arabia would gather coffee berries in Ethiopia believing they would help them survive their ordeal. This is perhaps how coffee beans first crossed the Red Sea and from there spread throughout the world.

In Middle Eastern countries coffee was considered to have medicinal properties and concoctions containing a large dose of caffeine were drunk as medicines before becoming an everyday beverage.

According to Islamic folk tales, Sheikh Omar was the first Arab to discover coffee and make a drink from the beans. He was a physician and man of God and was exiled to the desert region of Assab together with his followers for crimes against morality. In order to stave off the pangs of hunger, Omar and his companions collected the berries growing on an unknown shrub, boiled them and drank the infusion. It is said the idea came to them in a dream. The plant certainly helped a number of patients who had followed Omar into the desert in order to continue their treatment. When they returned to Mocha, their hometown, the former exiles told of the wonderful properties of this new beverage. A monastery was built in honour of Omar and he was proclaimed the city's patron.

It is also said that this energizing beverage was known to the Sufis, (ascetics who lived in the Yemeni desert regions in southern Arabia) who drank coffee to remain alert during their long gatherings, when

Above: the legend of the shepherd Kaldi; ancient parchment, Addis Ababa, Ethiopia.
Right: illustration of a branch from a coffee shrub, from a herbarium, ca 1800.

they would perform rituals celebrating the glory of God sometimes lasting over seven hundred nights. During the daylight hours, devotees would enjoy a coffee with their friends and benefit from the stimulating effects of the caffeine. Thus were the first coffee houses born.

HISTORY

There is really only one thing of which we can be reasonably sure: the coffee plant is native to Ethiopia. Its origins lies in the wonderful *coffee forest* in the Abyssinian region of Kaffa, lying between 900 and 2000 metres above sea level. In the prosperous province of Sidamo, in southern Ethiopia, the ancestors of the present-day nomadic mountain peoples of the Galla tribe were well aware of the invigorating effects of the coffee bean. It seems they crushed them and mixed them with animal fat to make a sort of energizing dietary supplement.

At the beginning of the sixteenth century coffee began to spread from the Yemeni monasteries to the big cities (Cairo in the first instance), attracting enthusiasts from all walks of life. So popular did the "black beverage" become that, in around 1523, a clause was added to marriage agreements in Turkey to the effect that it was the husband's responsibility to ensure his wife had an appropriate amount of coffee, on pain of divorce.

The Arabs tried for a long time to hold tight to their monopoly of the coffee trade, but keeping an eye on the millions of pilgrims making their way to Mecca every year was virtually impossible. It was one of these, by the name of Baba Budan, who swallowed seven red berries in 1670 and later planted them on his land in the Chandragiri Hills in Karnataka, in southern India. The result was so astonishing that the area was renamed in his honour and Baba Budan was proclaimed a saint thanks to his contribution to his country's prosperity. That moment marked the end to the Yemen's and to Arabia's monopoly over coffee.

Dutch traders, who since the early seventeenth century had been exporting all manner of wares (incense, sandalwood, silk, etc.) from Africa and Asia, immediately understood the potential offered by this new product and were keen to make its cultivation still more widespread. During the eighteenth century suitable regions governed by European powers were turned over to coffee cultivation. The world's first plantations sprang up in the equator region, not only in Ceylon and Java, but also in Sumatra, Celebes, Timor and Bali.

The story of the arrival of coffee in Martinique is perhaps the most romantic of all. It all began when, in the early eighteenth century, the Dutch presented a strong,

It was very fashionable to enjoy a cup of steaming coffee in 18th-century high society.

healthy coffee plant to the French government. The story goes that in his determination to transport the precious plant from France to Martinique without mishap, Captain Gabriel de Clieu assiduously shared with his ward his tiny water ration on the ship, managing in this way to let it survive the endless voyage.

Captain de Clieu introduced coffee growing to the French colonies in around 1723. Most of the world's present crop is probably ultimately derived from that one plant.

In a short time coffee became such a precious commodity that people would go to any lengths to get their hands on it. In 1727 a dispute arose between France and the Dutch colonists in Guyana, and the Portuguese Francisco de Melo Palheta was invited to arbitrate. He seized this opportunity to pilfer a few of the highly sought-after beans. But in the end it was only thanks to a woman's love that he was able to bring his scheme to a successful conclusion. On the day of his departure, his ladylove presented him with a large bunch of flowers with the bright cherries peeping out from among the blooms. He planted them in Para, in Brazil, thus becoming the first person to produce coffee for a world market.

Above: a Cairo *coffee house*, Konstantin Makovsky, ca 1870-1879.

Double page overleaf: the initial legs of the coffee plant's voyage around the world, which began in Ethiopia and ended back on the African continent.

NOVA TOTIVS TE[

MARTINIQUE

GUYANA

1727

BRAZIL

VM ORBIS TABVLA.

FRANCE

1670

EGYPT
14TH CENTURY
YEMEN   INDIA

CEYLON
SUMATRA
KENYA

17TH CENTURY   JAVA
BALI
TIMOR

0TH CENTURY

THE SPREAD OF COFFEE AND COFFEE HOUSES

Travellers and traders who criss-crossed the oceans soon became aware of coffee's huge popularity in the Islamic world and were not slow to bring the news back to Europe, enthusing about the beverage in pages upon pages of prose and drawings.

Coffee houses soon became synonymous with friendship and conviviality, where people could relax and keep up with the latest political gossip. The first coffee house opened in 1554 in Istanbul, then more commonly known as Constantinople, the former Byzantium. Coffee shops were actually called *mektebi-irfan*, or "schools of the cultured", because men would spend time in these places to swap and discuss the news.

However, it appears that, in what is now Yemen, it had been common practice for at least a century to sip a coffee now and again and that the government was all in favour of its consumption, praising coffee's estimable qualities.

Coffee quickly won over the Arab peoples, especially in view of the Koran's ban on the consumption of any alcoholic drink. The "wine of Islam" (as it was nicknamed) began to spread along the Red Sea coast and inland to Mecca, Medina and Cairo. According to some accounts, coffee was viewed favourably by Islam because it stimulated the intelligence, the imagination and the creative impulse, unlike wine which was thought to make men sleepy and cause minds to wander. Islam was quick to welcome new converts and was just as eager to introduce newly conquered lands to the delights of coffee.

The year 1615 is traditionally regarded as the date when coffee first appeared in Europe, brought by Venetian merchants along the trade routes linking Venice and Naples to the East. The first to describe the coffee plant was a certain Prospero Alpino, a physician who had lived in Egypt as an aide to the Venetian consul. In his *De Plantis Aegypti*, a treatise on North African plants published in 1592, coffee is prominent and its characteristics are discussed with the help of accurate and detailed drawings and comments about methods of pollination. Alpino was the first to mention an example of an autogamous (self-fertilizing) plant.

The great Swedish botanist Linnaeus, the father of the modern system of taxonomy, later named the shrub *Coffea arabica* in 1753.

Although discovered at a later date, *Coffea canephora*, better known as Robusta, enjoys an equally fascinating history. In 1857 two English explorers, Richard Burton and John Speake came across this new species of coffee plant on an expedition to find the source of the Nile. Tougher, hence the name, and far more resistant to the parasites and diseases that plagued Arabica, this new Robusta coffee soon became popular and was introduced around the world alongside, or instead of its cousin, quickly increasing the yield. At this time the coffee trade was firmly in the hands of the colonial powers, since the vast majority of plantations were in territories under their rule. This meant that Ethiopian coffee was shipped to Italy, West African coffee went to France and East African coffee made the journey to England. The United States had their own source in South America.

When it first reached Italy, in the early seventeenth century, coffee in fact found a number of obstacles barring its way. The Church was particularly wary of welcoming a new product from Muslim lands. Then there was the danger of patrons frequenting the new coffee houses, considered dens of perdition, altogether too assiduously for their own good. Even so, Pope Clement VIII chose to taste this "Devil's drink" before pronouncing his anathema, and he enjoyed it so much that he decided to sanctify the beverage, declaring that it was so delicious that it would be a crime to leave it to the unbelievers.

London *coffee houses* were a favourite haunt of the English nobility, where they would discuss art, politics and business while drinking coffee and smoking a pipe; oil painting, English school, ca 1700.

From the mid seventeenth century and with the Pope's blessing coffee took its place on Italian hawkers' stands next to the other great novelty of the age, chocolate, and other favourites like lemonade and spirits. So, elegant coffee houses began to sprout up both in Venice and in other large cities (for example, Caffé Greco in Rome, Pedrocchi in Padua, San Carlo in Turin and many others).

The boom in coffee consumption became a real craze and *coffee houses* spread from England to Austria, Holland, France and Germany, becoming focal points of town life. In England there sprang up the curious *"penny universities"*, so named because for one *penny* you could have a cup of coffee and take part in interesting and impassioned discussions. By the mid seventeenth century there were over three hundred *coffee houses* in London, many of which enjoyed the patronage of merchants, shipowners, stockbrokers, and artists – the people who animated the country's economic and cultural life. History is full of businessmen who cut their teeth wheeling and dealing in London coffee houses: Lloyd's of London, one of the largest insurance companies in the world was created in the very *coffee house* run by Edward Lloyd.

In the same century coffee houses were taken across the Atlantic by the English and found equal favour in what was first called new Amsterdam and later renamed New York. But popular as the coffee houses were, tea was still the favourite beverage of the New World, until the colonists rose in rebellion against the exorbitant taxes levied on tea by King George III. The Boston tea party, as the event became known, marked a permanent change in America's taste. Ever since, coffee has been the favourite beverage in the United States.

An episode during the Boston Tea Party. In 1773 English settlers rose up in rebellion at the exorbitant taxes imposed by George III, and threw all the cases of the precious, newly arrived tea into the sea; 18th-century watercolour print.

WHICH COFFEE: ARABICA OR ROBUSTA?

The coffee plant is an evergreen shrub of the family *Rubiacee* which thrives up to an altitude of 2000-2500 metres in the tropical belt around the planet. The fruit takes the form of a drupe, often referred to as a cherry, containing two seeds wrapped in a membrane (the parchment) and a layer of sugary flesh, the mucilage. The seeds are oval in shape, with a centre cut down the middle, and turn into coffee beans as they ripen.

Coffea arabica and *Coffea canephora* (better known as Robusta) are native to the forests of Africa and are the main species used in the commercial production of coffee throughout the world. In fact, there are other plants with similar seeds, but it has not proved possible to produce anything drinkable from them.

The two species differ in the shape of the bean: the Arabica is flatter and longer, with a sinuous centre cut, while Robusta strains are convex, rounded and have a straighter centre cut. The caffeine content is also different: an espresso made with a blend of pure Arabica contains 40 to 65

Above: section of a freshly-picked Brazilian *Coffea arabica* cherry, showing the skin and the layer of sugary pulp enveloping the two coffee beans lying side by side.

Facing page: *Coffea arabica* shrub in a Colombian plantation, in the Popayan region.

milligrams of caffeine, while Robusta has around double the amount (80 to 120 milligrams). Arabica blends produce a coffee with good acidity, a subtle aroma and a caramel aftertaste. Robusta lends a certain body to the drink, but the aroma is rather flat and tends to be woody and not to everyone's taste.

ARABICA

Characteristics:

oval bean with
a sinuous centre cut
more widespread
less bitter
more aromatic
more subtle
less astringent
caffeine 0.8-1.5%
55-60% of world production

ROBUSTA

Characteristics:
round bean and
straight centre cut
hardier
more bitter
more full-bodied
caffeine 1.7-3.5%
40-45% of world production

Facing page: coffee blossoms. These highly scented flowers measure around one and a half centimetres and bloom after every significant rainfall.

CULTIVATION: FROM SOIL TO HARVEST

Coffee plantations around the world are situated in tropical Africa, Asia and America, where its ideal climatic conditions can be found: a temperature ranging from 17 to 30 degrees centigrade and annual rainfall of between 1200 and 2000 millimetres, in clearly distinct rainy periods (annual rainfall in Italy is around 1000 millimetres). Coffee requires soil rich in humus, nitrogen and potassium and grows at an altitude of up to 2500 metres.

The shrub is grown to a height of two to three metres in plantations, to make cultivation and harvesting as simple as possible. Dead wood is removed and pruning encourages new growth, as well as ensuring good ventilation and the optimal level of natural light.

Regular fertilization and irrigation provide the coffee plant with the proper nutrition and right amount of water.

Facing page: *Coffea arabica* seedlings just after germination in a Brazilian greenhouse.

Above: coffee seedlings with their first two leaves, known as cotyledons, in a Colombian nursery. At this stage they need to be protected from direct sunlight.

SOWING

Coffee cultivation begins with the seed and a properly organised nursery. Firstly, only ripe cherries are suitable, their fleshy mucilage is removed and they are put out to dry in the shade or dried artificially. Coffee seeds germinate only if they are sown up to eight weeks after being harvested. They are placed in special sand "beds" in a nursery, at a depth of one or two centimetres.

The seedlings sprout after 8-10 weeks and as soon as the two typical, perfectly shaped light green leaves (known as cotyledons) appear, they are immediately transferred to special soft plastic containers, which are in turn carefully arranged in new "beds" in rows, around 20-25 centimetres apart.

The plants spend twelve months in greenhouses or places protected from direct sunlight (only six months in Brazil, in view of the intensive cultivation), until they are 30-50 cm high. At this point they can be transplanted to their final destination: the coffee plantation proper.

This technique is most common in Central America, Brazil and India, where the wide-open spaces make it possible to use large machinery and irrigation systems. In African countries, such as Ethiopia, Uganda and Zaire, the seedlings grow spontaneously or with a minimum of help during sowing. At all events, the soil in which they grow is extremely important and has to be well aerated and drained, for the roots of the young coffee plant require a plentiful supply of oxygen.

The traditional and earliest method of growing coffee is the so-called *consociational* system, which is still practised in parts of Central America and India: *coffee* plants grow together with other, taller crops (such as mango, banana, citrus fruits and pepper), which provide them with natural protection from the sun's rays. It's a little like older brothers looking after their younger siblings. Tall plants with

Above: coffee plants being bedded out in a plantation, next to tall-growing trees which will shade them as they grow.

thick, strong trunks shelter the precious beans below from the wind and plants with large leaves offer them shade from the sun.

The *intensive* system favoured in Brazil is a monoculture involving a large number of coffee plants grown at high density and it requires the help of systems of irrigation and mechanization. This entails considerable investments and provides a high yield, but also has a greater impact on the environment.

Coffee plants begin to fruit after two or three years and the number of years they continue to bear fruit depends on the techniques of cultivation. In intensive cultivation the plants are exploited for all they can give and last around fifteen years. But in India, for instance, the extensive plantations enable the plant to live longer and provide a crop for up to fifty years.

Two ways to ensure coffee plants receive the right amount of water. Left: in Colombia (San Gil) it rains frequently and the soil is kept moist thanks to the tall trees shading the plantation. In Brazil's Minas Gerais plateau (right) rain is scarcer and mechanical irrigation is required.

HARVESTING

Coffee grows in the planet's tropical regions, where the climate is characterised by hot, dry seasons alternating with rainy seasons. The plant flowers after every significant rainfall and this means that every plant has flowers and fruit at different stages of ripeness. This naturally makes harvesting a complicated business. For a good-quality coffee it is essential to choose only fully ripe fruit, since beans from unripe cherries can give the final coffee a woody, astringent taste. Cherries that are overripe can also spoil a coffee, giving it rancid or rotten undertones.

The cherries ripen eight to nine months after the flowers first appear on the plant and are perfect when they are shiny, red and still firm to the touch. Three different types of harvesting methods can be used, according to the country and the type of coffee desired.

Selective *picking* is used, for example, in Central America, Ethiopia, Kenya and India and entails the pickers walking among the plants at regular intervals picking the cherries one by one and selecting only those which have reached the right degree of ripeness. This is obviously a slow and expensive method but provides an excellent quality coffee.

Stripping can be performed either by hand or mechanically and in this case, as the term suggests, all the cherries are removed from the branches irrespective of their ripeness and the selection is carried out later. This process is clearly not as discriminating as selective *picking* and requires further sorting later. Big basins full of water are often used to make the sorting easier, as ripe and unripe cherries have different buoyancies.

Mechanical *stripping* is most commonly used in Brazil. Plantations need to be flat so that the large machines can move between the plants. The branches are gently shaken by flexible rods adjusted so that only the ripest cherries drop off and the plant is not damaged in any way.

The three methods of picking ripe cherries.

Left: selective *picking* is performed by hand and the picker is careful to choose only ripe cherries (Colombia, Popayan); right: manual *stripping* (Brazil, São Gotardo); far right: mechanical *stripping* carried out with wheeled vehicles, which shake the branches with flexible rods adjusted for strength and number of vibrations so that only the ripest cherries drop off (Brazil, Monte Carmelo).

PROCESSING IN THE COUNTRIES OF ORIGIN

There can be no short cuts in how and when the processing performed immediately after harvesting is carried out. The coffee bean needs the tender loving care that a mother would give to her newborn. It has to be helped through each of the subsequent stages, until at last it is put in a ship to release its aroma in some far-off land. The final result in the cup depends in large degree on this process.

The beans have to be extracted from the cherries within a few hours of harvesting by removing the flesh and the skin, otherwise the cherries could begin to ferment or rot, giving the coffee an unpleasant taste.

There are basically two systems for extracting coffee beans, but before this is done the cherries have to be separated from any foreign objects, such as pebbles, leaves and twigs by being sieved or with the aid of air jets.

Facing page: in Pocos de Caldas, in Brazil, sieves are used in some plantations to separate cherries from leaves, twigs and any stones or clods of earth.

Above: in the Monte Carmelo region of Brazil coffee beans are laid out to dry on huge threshing floors. The beans are constantly turned over to ensure uniform drying, often using wooden rakes drawn by horses.

In *dry processing* the cherries are dried in the open on special patios and provide the so-called "natural coffees". A layer of cherries no higher than 2-3 centimetres is spread out and turned over frequently (up to 15-20 times a day) so that they retain an even humidity throughout. They are then put into mechanical driers operating at a maximum temperature of 35-40 degrees to complete and speed up the drying process.

In *wet processing*, resulting in "washed coffees", the skin and part of the flesh of the cherry are removed inside drums known as depulpers. The seeds are then left to ferment (for a number of hours) in large containers in order to remove the slimy layer of sugary mucilage still clinging to the bean.

A third method is also worth mentioning, which could be said to lie between the dry processing and the wet. This is the so-called *descascado* approach typical of Brazil. The flesh is removed from the

Above: ripe cherries. Unripe and fermented cherries have been removed using water by exploiting their different specific weight and thus different buoyancy.

Facing page: left, freshly-picked cherries are poured into a depulping machine which uses an endless screw (right) to eliminate the skin and part of the pulp, leaving the coffee bean bare.

cherries, but instead of letting the beans ferment, they are left in the sun to dry without any further processing.

At the end of the procedure, whichever method is used, the drupes have been turned into green coffee. The beans are then sorted by size and carefully selected, to ensure the final product is of the highest quality.

Dried coffee beans.

Parchment, the membrane enveloping the bean.

Beans with the parchment removed.

TRANSPORT

The journey a coffee bean has to make is extremely long and tricky, with hazardous lands and oceans to cross and considerable variations in temperature to overcome.

Coffee is normally packed in sixty-kilo sacks of jute (a natural material that lets the contents of the sack breathe). Each sack has the weight, provenance and port of embarkation stamped on it. The coffee is stored in a dry and very well ventilated location, if possible in sacks.

The beans are transported by sea, truck or rail and about 95% reach Europe in containers, which can be of two types: standard containers, with unlined wooden bottoms, and refrigerated containers, which are not as yet so commonly used. In order to preserve the quality of the beans, it is extremely important to protect them from the rain, damp, cold and excessive heat.

The chief ports of arrival are Trieste, Antwerp, Barcelona, Bremen, Hamburg, Le Havre, London, Rotterdam, New Orleans, Genoa, New York, Miami and Houston.

The import-export business is controlled mainly by large international trading companies, which deal in very large quantities of coffee, following it through the various processing stages: they are in a position to offer their customers a broad range of services, including processing in the coffee's place of origin, warehousing, roasting and grinding.

COFFEE'S JOURNEYS

It's a long time since coffee beans found their way across Ethiopia in some scruffy pouch and were introduced to Arabian lands. As the popularity of this black beverage gathered pace in Europe, the endless journeys across land gave way to transport by sea.

It would seem that the earliest document describing these wanderings of the green coffee bean is *Mercure Galant*, published in Paris in 1696, which pointed to Jedda in western Saudi Arabia as the port of embarkation of beans grown around Mecca. From there they were shipped to Suez, unloaded and carried by camel to Alexandria, where Venetian and French ships were waiting to forward the cargo to Europe, the former to Venice and the latter to Marseille.

The first great coffee route therefore undoubtedly crossed the eastern Mediterranean. When the Dutch set up the first plantations in Java and Sumatra in the early eighteenth century, ships employed in the spice trade supplemented their cargo with bags of the precious new crop. This journey was much longer and more demanding than the former and meant sailing right round the African continent, including the treacherous Cape of Good Hope.

In that same period, new routes were opened, from Central and South America, carrying beans

Facing page: after a hard day's work in the huge coffee plantations, a lorry in Hassor in Karnataka, southern India, takes pickers to centres where they will be able to sell their crop.

cultivated in Martinique, Guyana, Brazil, Jamaica and Mexico. English and Portuguese ships could be found on both the Far Eastern and American routes, while the French narrowed their efforts to the eastern trade and the Spanish to the western.

Today, the traditional Middle and Far Eastern trade routes and Central and South American ones have been joined by the East and West African routes transporting coffee from Ethiopia, Kenya, Tanzania and Madagascar on one side and Ivory Coast, Cameroon and Zaire on the other. The opening of the Suez Canal was a tremendous help in this regard as it enabled ships to shorten their voyages considerably and thus reduce costs.

Above, from left: sacks of coffee being unloaded from the hold of a ship and port vehicles in operation, port of Trieste, 1930.

The adventurous journeys of the coffee bean began in the eighteenth century in majestic sailing ships and now involve more mundane, massive container ships, which are able to transport sacks of beans from the Americas to Europe in under two weeks. Freight costs are still huge, sometimes doubling the cost of the cargo they are carrying. This is why alternatives have been explored, such as filling the holds directly with green coffee beans rather than carefully loading the traditional jute sacks. However, this approach forfeits any chance of ensuring the quality of the product on arrival, as a little water seeping in can ruin the entire contents of the container.

Above: one of the warehouses in the port of Cartagena (Colombia), on the Caribbean Sea. This is one of the most important entrepots in South America, handling large quantities of coffee, tobacco, oil, rubber and cotton. Coffee is sent here from all coffee growing areas and stored in jute sacks away from direct sunlight and humidity before being loaded into containers and shipped to Europe.

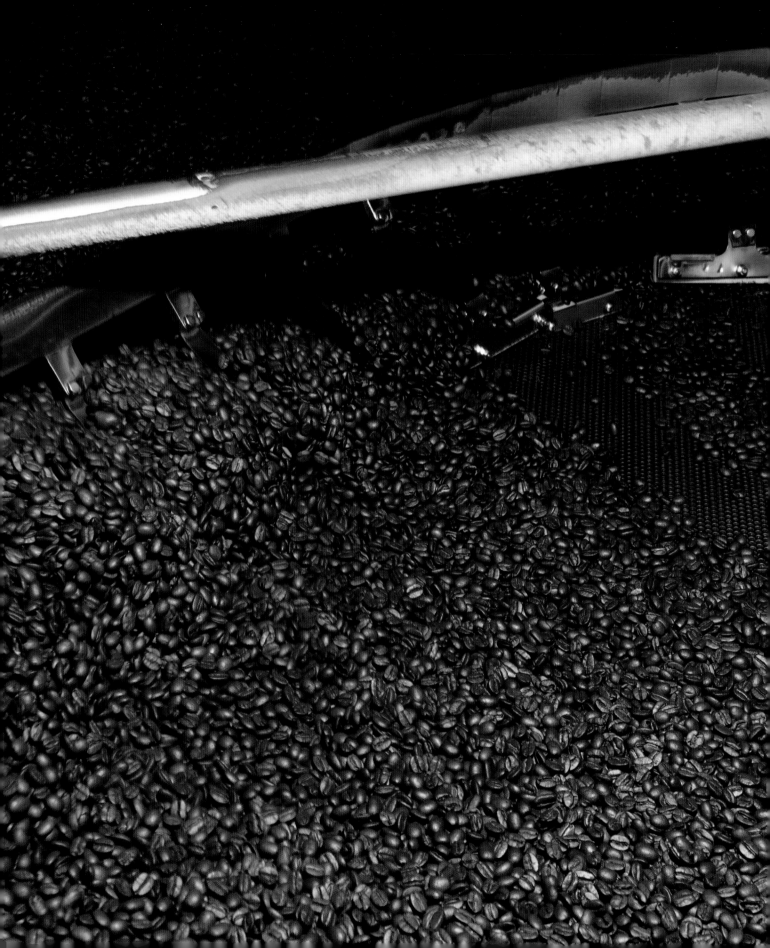

THE ART OF ROASTING COFFEE BEANS

Coffee beans reach Europe green and before they can be used they have to be roasted.

Roasting is the most important part of the processing, since only by being roasted can coffee release the properties that make it distinctive in the cup. During this process, chemical and physical reactions produce over one thousand substances, all of which contribute to the coffee's final taste and aroma. The cycle takes around a quarter of an hour, as the beans are heated according to a specific temperature curve, rising gradually to 200-230 degrees centigrade.

There are three phases in the roasting process: drying, which eliminates any residual humidity in the green beans, roasting proper, and cooling.

The drying phase accounts for almost half the entire process. It is important to work with batches that have an even degree of humidity throughout so that the roasting is uniform.

The bean decreases in weight by 16% during roasting, and its volume increases by 60%. The sugars are caramelised, the water evaporates and reactions between the

| Green Arabica | Roasted Arabica | Green Robusta | Roasted Robusta |

Left: when roasting is complete, the coffee beans have to be quickly cooled to prevent them charring and turning bitter. The beans are constantly tossed around, while a flow of cold air blows through them from little holes in the bottom of the cooling pan.

sugars and proteins in the bean create the pigments that give it its characteristic dark brown colour and develop the aromas (the 200-300 found in the green bean increase to over 1,000 in the roasted version).

Rapid cooling of the hot beans completes the process and can be done using two different methods: water or air cooling.

Water cooling is the quicker method but may lead to a loss of aromas, not to mention that coffee beans tend to absorb large amounts of water, leading to a less satisfying cup. Air cooling ensures that the properties of a batch of coffee beans are better preserved.

But why is roasting considered an art?

The coffee's final taste and aroma depend on the temperature curve in the roasting process, namely the skill displayed in adjusting the temperature over time. Every roasting follows its own specially devised curve. Different curves produce coffees designed to suit the requirements and tastes of different customers. Lower temperatures provide a coffee which is lighter in colour, not very bitter and with a pleasing degree of acidity. Higher temperatures give a darker, pleasantly bitter coffee with a fuller, more intense flavour. But it is essential not to over-roast the beans, as they can be charred and the batch to all intents and purposes ruined.

The roasting process can vary considerably according to the country where the coffee is to be drunk.

Lightly roasted coffees tend to be preferred in Finland and northern Europe in general. In the cup, the coffee is light, with little body and tending towards acid rather than bitter.

In Germany and the United States the taste is for a slightly darker roast; they say that the colour should be that of a monk's habit. Coffees made with these beans are still rather light, but a little less acid and more bitter.

The so-called continental roast, found in France and northern Italy, seeks a perfect balance between acidity and bitterness.

Lastly, the dark roast, beloved of Neapolitans and Spaniards, results in a very dark, pleasantly bitter and full-bodied coffee.

Beans, life size

Above: the time spent roasting is the most important quarter of an hour in a bean's life. Around one thousand substances, all contributing to the coffee's final taste and aroma, develop in just a few minutes. The weight decreases by 16%, while the volume increases by 60%. The picture above shows fourteen photos of coffee beans at different moments in the roasting process.

Facing page: after roasting and cooling, the beans are sucked up into this transparent tube. The flow of air from below ensures that any small stones remain at the bottom.

Coffee and us

WHY DO WE DRINK IT?

The smell, the aroma, the whole *experience* of drinking coffee have turned a simple beverage into an icon of modern living and of our culture. More and more people all over the world love to begin their day with a steaming cup of coffee. The ritual changes according to where one lives. A few simple gestures, differing from espresso to, say, filter coffee, but with the same aim: to create a little oasis for oneself, to start the day with energy and in good spirits.

But coffee is good not only for the spirit: it gives us a lift and can be beneficial for our health, too. It is a source of wisdom rather than nourishment, a useful rite in strengthening bonds, making new friends, extending deals and prompting thoughts.

Coffee has been drunk in Europe since the beginning of the seventeenth century. Strange as it may seem today, the ancient world and medieval Europe had no stimulating "magic potion" and certainly felt no need for one.

Between the mid-seventeenth and mid-nineteenth centuries something occurred that made coffee particularly desirable and even indispensable: the so-called Little Ice Age, which gradually spread across the whole of Europe causing famines, freezing winters and cold summers. Tea and coffee helped ward off the pangs of hunger and warmed the body and this increased consumption enormously, until the pair became the most popular drinks in the world.

Facing page: a quick coffee in a bar in 1955.

Aside from the characteristics of the climate, the Middle Ages were a time when life was lived slowly. There were a lot of holy days and society was not very well organised. An important turning point occurred in 1583, when Galileo Galilei formulated the law governing the movement of the pendulum. This was a real revolution and led to the invention of clockwork mechanisms. In the second half of the seventeenth century, the minute-hand became common in England and this newly-acquired accuracy ushered in economic and industrial enterprises that were unthinkable only a few years before.

It may be only a coincidence, but this new way of thinking and behaving took root at precisely the time when coffee drinking was becoming popular in Venice, Paris, Amsterdam, London and throughout Europe. The invigorating effects of coffee helped provide the energy to overcome the grindingly long hours of work and stave off exhaustion.

In this period, a good cup of coffee became an essential tonic for the body, as well as an irreplaceable pick-me-up, enabling people to keep alert and ready to face the many challenges of a busy life. It therefore makes sense to surmise that the invention of the pocket watch and the discovery of the beneficial effects of caffeine formed a providential combination for the development of the modern world.

As Benjamin Franklin observed, the introduction of coffee from the distant American colonies into smart circles in London was a godsend for the times. One of its great merits was that the alluringly fragrant black beverage has not a drop of alcohol in it, a real blessing in an age ravaged by the scourge of alcoholism.

Coffee was therefore welcomed as an encouragement to sobriety and as an elixir that could be consumed upon waking and throughout the day, freeing mankind from the clutches of the demon drink and the drunken debauchery it occasioned. The authorities were therefore quick to give tea and coffee their fullest backing, in view of their contribution to the productivity that the newly competitive mechanized age demanded.

The industrial revolution saw the development of a process which, especially in England, led to the transition from a basically agricultural and trading economy to a modern industrial society, with reliance on machinery powered by energy derived from fossil fuels.

The fact that these new factory workers took a liking to coffee meant they gradually turned away from the ubiquitous beer and it made the transfer from field to factory less stressful. When millions found themselves swapping a life spent immersed in nature for one governed by the clock, it was natural that many clutched at whatever could help them cope.

Coffee became an invaluable ally in the struggle against dozing off while at the machines during the endless shifts on the production line. It seems safe to assume that the consumption of food and drink containing caffeine, together with the invention of electric light in the same period, helped people adapt to the new rhythms of work regulated by the hands of the clock rather than the rising and setting of the sun.

Another point that should not be overlooked in view of the period is that water always had to be boiled when making tea or coffee, thus diminishing the incidence of gastrointestinal diseases, which were very common among factory workers living in insalubrious and overcrowded cities.

Caffeine, therefore, had a crucial role during the first economic boom in history. It is tempting to agree with Charles Czeisler, a sleep expert at Harvard Medical School, when the neurologist says that caffeine made the modern world possible: "Without the aid of coffee, the frenzied pace of modern society would not exist, with its twenty-four hour working days".

But coffee also turned into a cultural symbol. One of the first *coffee houses* in Europe, founded by Edward Lloyd, opened in London in 1688: a meeting place for traders and sailors, it was the core of what later developed into one of the leading insurance companies in the world.

In this way coffee houses gradually spread as lively meeting places for conducting business and discussing art, science and literature. In Paris in particular the first coffee houses became a symbol of the Enlightenment.

Above: coffee being handed out to the destitute at the Water Street Mission, in Ireland, ca 1880.

CAFFEINE
AND ITS CHARACTERISTICS

Caffeine has always existed. It is an alkaloid (i.e. an organic substance) found in the leaves, seeds or fruit of over fifty species of plant, including tea, coffee, cocoa and cola.

The invigorating potential of this substance was already well known in the sixth century BC, when it was first used by the father of Chinese Taoism Lao-Tzu, who advised his followers to drink tea as an elixir of long life.

The story of the discovery of caffeine in the West is one of those strange tales hovering between legend and reality.

It was in 1819, when the fashion for *coffee shops* was burgeoning throughout Western Europe, that the German physician Friedlieb Ferdinand Runge received a small box containing a few precious Arabian coffee beans from Johann Wolfgang Goethe, with the request that he analyse them. Goethe, who took an amateur's delight in studying biology, chemistry and mineralogy, was curious to find out what it was about coffee that made it so popular in all the drawing rooms of the period.

Flattered, Runge set to work and managed to isolate a substance he called *Kaffebase*. The term caffeine was probably actually coined by the physicist Theodor Fechner who, a few years after Runge, described the same substance, calling it *coffein*.

By the end of the century caffeine had also been discovered in cola and cocoa nuts.

Shall we take a close-up of caffeine? This is the best known of all coffee's components and is known among chemists by the pompous name of 1.3.7-trimethylxanthine. However, it also has a number of aliases: theine, mateine and guaranine, but it is always the same molecule belonging to the family of purine alkaloids, along with a number of others like theophylline (the active ingredient in tea) and theobromine (found in cocoa).

Caffeine is made up of four of the most common elements on Earth: carbon, hydrogen, nitrogen and oxygen. When extracted from coffee it takes the form of a white powder like cornstarch. Although basically flavourless, it is very slightly bitter.

How much caffeine can we drink in a day? The consensus among scientists is that 300-400 milligrams can be considered a moderate amount.

However, it is crucial to bear in mind that caffeine is not found only in coffee, but is also present in tea, cocoa, maté and guarana, as well as many soft drinks.

Above: in front of the chemical laboratories in the town of Oranienburg, Germany, stands a statue of the German physician Friedlieb Ferdinand Runge, who isolated a substance he called *Kaffeebase*, that is, caffeine, in 1819.

Facing page: caffeine crystals under the optical microscope.

Double page overleaf: caffeine crystals in the foam of an espresso, enlarged under an optical microscope.

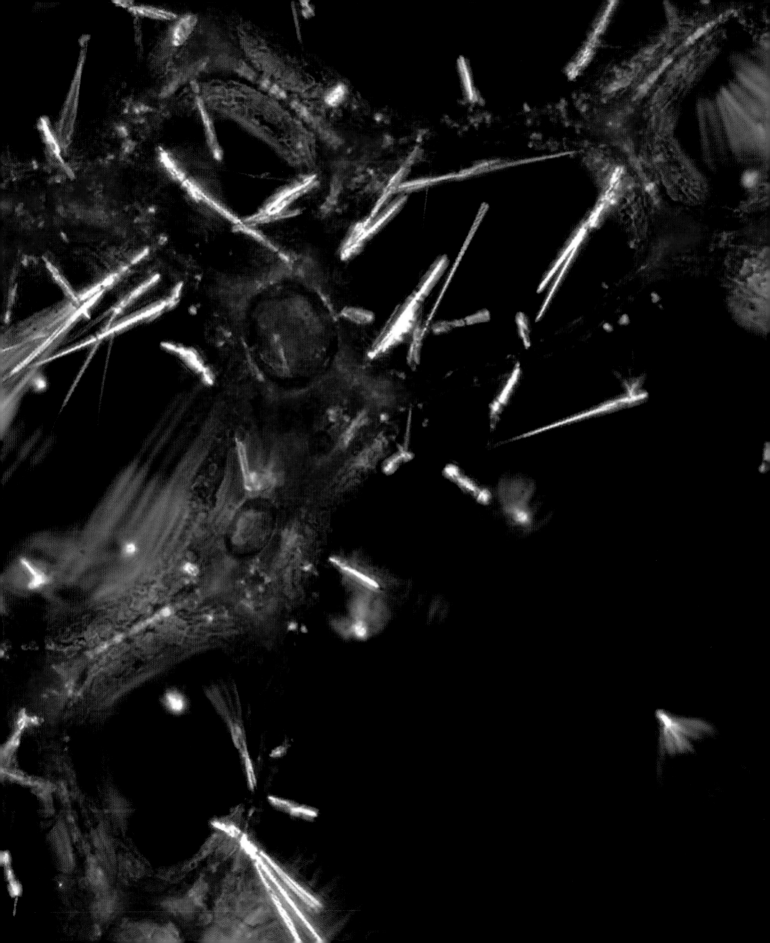

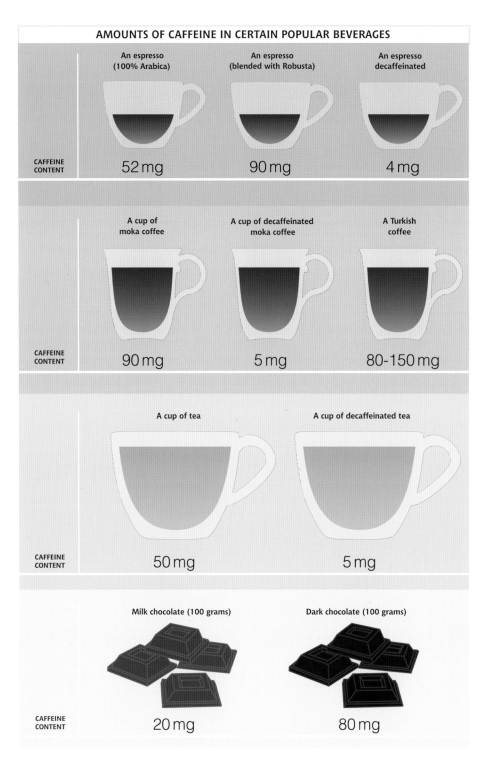

AMOUNTS OF CAFFEINE IN CERTAIN POPULAR BEVERAGES

An espresso (100% Arabica)	An espresso (blended with Robusta)	An espresso decaffeinated
CAFFEINE CONTENT 52 mg	90 mg	4 mg

A cup of moka coffee	A cup of decaffeinated moka coffee	A Turkish coffee
CAFFEINE CONTENT 90 mg	5 mg	80-150 mg

A cup of tea	A cup of decaffeinated tea
CAFFEINE CONTENT 50 mg	5 mg

Milk chocolate (100 grams)	Dark chocolate (100 grams)
CAFFEINE CONTENT 20 mg	80 mg

And as far as coffee is concerned, the amount present depends on the variety of bean used and the way it is prepared.

Arabica and Robusta beans differ in the quality and quantity of the chemical compounds in their raw beans. For instance, Arabica contains less caffeine (around half of the Robusta content).

In order to put the amounts in some perspective, the caffeine content of various common beverages will be compared. It is important to bear in mind that a full flavour does not necessarily indicate a high caffeine content.

Facing page: coarse caffeine crystals just extracted from coffee beans; in the glass container, refined caffeine crystals.

Caffeine crystals are highly soluble in hot water and the percentage extracted in the coffee depends on a range of variables:

DOSE	the more the coffee, the more the caffeine
TYPE OF PREPARATION	infusion (used in Turkish coffee, for example) releases more caffeine than percolation (espresso and moka)
WATER TEMPERATURE	the higher the temperature, the more caffeine is extracted
PREPARATION TIME	longer processes extract more caffeine
FINAL VOLUME	obviously, the overall amount of caffeine depends on the volume of coffee in the cup

Espresso coffee has the lowest percentage of caffeine for any given blend: around 75% is extracted from roasted beans, as against 98% in American coffee. This is due to the briefer contact, the lower water temperature and the smaller volume of coffee in the cup.

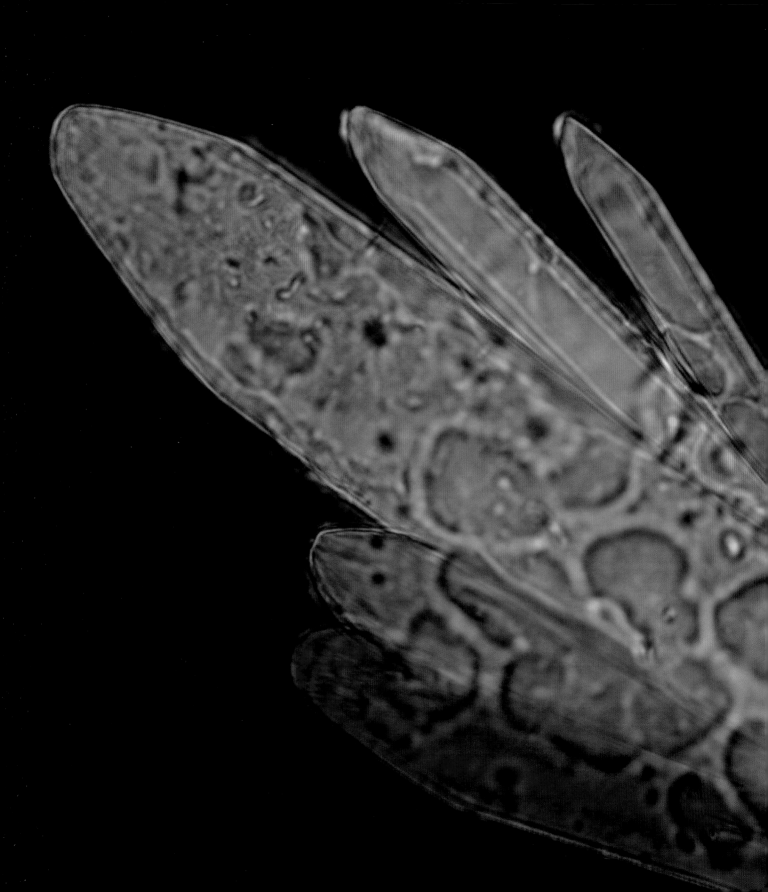

COFFEE AND OUR HEALTH

Every day, almost a billion people drink at least one cup of coffee and a proportion of these probably wonder if this habit is good for them. Thousands of studies have proved conclusively that if drunk in moderation (four or five cups of espresso a day), coffee does no harm at all.

When considering the physical effects of drinking coffee, one should be aware first of all that the most recent and most accredited medical literature on the topic has downplayed beliefs commonly held in the past about the ill effects of coffee. For example, coffee is no longer held responsible for heart conditions, various types of cancer, difficult pregnancies and impaired breastfeeding, osteoporosis and hypercholesterolemia.

The effects of coffee drinking on people's health began to be a topic of serious research in the eighties. The result was a (largely predictable) rehabilitation of coffee and the return to commonsense after a lot of scaremongering stories about the noxious potential of one its chief components, caffeine.

So one should be careful of misinterpreting experimental data and of associating caffeine exclusively with coffee. First of all, due weight should be given to the type of coffee drunk: as mentioned, an espresso taken in a bar contains less caffeine than an American filter coffee, in spite of the fact that people commonly associate a strong flavour with an equally stimulating effect.

Since caffeine is water soluble and passes through all cell membranes with ease, it is quickly and completely absorbed by the stomach and the upper digestive tract, where it is taken up by the blood stream and distributed to all the organs of the body.

Caffeine's presence in the body is short-lived and there is no danger of it accumulating. It quickly reaches its maximum concentration in the blood, then gradually diminishes and disappears within a few hours. In order to be able to compare results, scientific research uses the concept of half-life, referring to the time it takes to reduce by half the amount of any given substance in the blood; in the case of caffeine the average is around four hours.

Even so, it is important to know how much caffeine has been ingested, since it is the most commonly used pharmacologically active substance in the world. Its chief effect is to stimulate the central nervous system, influencing human behaviour and counteracting adenosine, a product produced by our metabolism that acts as a natural sleeping pill. This means that caffeine combats drowsiness and leads to increased alertness, stimulating the nervous system and uplifting our mood. It helps in breathing and in the digestive process and tends to reduce any pangs of hunger, which makes it a good ally in slimming diets.

Facing page: detail of a caffeine crystal considerably enlarged under an optical microscope.

COFFEE IN DAILY LIFE

One tends to attribute to this black beverage a property which is often the object of long discussions and... sleepless nights! It can be said here that, drunk according to one's needs and with an eye on the rhythms of one's body, coffee has no effect on sleep. However, consumed in excessive quantities (over seven cups a day), it can lead to problems in falling asleep and to curtailed sleep. At even higher doses (amounting to over one gram of caffeine), coffee can cause a sense of anxiety and uneasiness.

But there is absolutely no doubt that a coffee break helps to keep us alert and on the ball.

A good cup of coffee can help fight those bothersome symptoms that slow us down and make us inattentive, especially when having to work an unfamiliar shift.

Another quite straightforward, but equally important question often comes up: can coffee help in cases of headache?

Some studies suggest a small cup of coffee can slightly relieve migraine symptoms, thanks to the fact that vasoconstricting substances (like caffeine) have a beneficial effect in cases of pain due to enlarged blood vessels. Although not all headaches are of this type, it does no harm to see if a cup of coffee helps.

Left: coffee made with a moka.

Facing page: serving a coffee piping hot is often a sign of quality in Naples. This is why it is common practice to give fast, professional waiters a tip.

COFFEE AND ANTIOXIDANTS

In addition to caffeine, coffee also contains hundreds of different chemical substances. Looking at them in detail, one soon notices the surprising number of antioxidants included among them. There is much talk of antioxidants and free radicals in modern times, but not everyone knows exactly what these buzzwords mean and, above all, the effects these substances may have on our daily lives.

So, first of all, what are oxidants, commonly known as free radicals? Oxidants are oxygen compounds that lead to the process of oxidation (ageing) of our cells. Some sources of oxidants are cigarette smoke, lack of exercise, atmospheric pollution, the sun's rays and any inflammation of the tissues.

The body's natural defences can only do so much to protect us from this damage, which has repercussions on ageing, cardiovascular diseases, the possible development of cancers and the general

undermining of the immune system. Much research has been prompted by the desire to better understand the links between oxidants and certain types of disease.

A healthy, balanced diet provides us with antioxidants, thus helping to prevent, or at least delay and mitigate the worst of these degenerative conditions.

Antioxidants therefore inhibit the action of free radicals and help counter the damage caused by oxidation. The human body has its own complex array of natural antioxidants, but a proper diet can provide an invaluable boost. For example, vitamins E and C, beta-carotene, selenium, uric acid and certain other proteins all combat free radicals and help reduce their numbers. Soya, green and black tea, red wine, rosemary, citrus fruits, onions, olives and vegetables of the cauliflower and broccoli family are just some of the foodstuffs high in antioxidants. Our defences against free radicals can thus be reinforced by a diet rich in these ingredients, among which coffee also has its place.

As has been proved in numerous studies, including a series carried out by Professor D'Amicis, head of the Nutritional Documentation and Information Unit, at IN-RAN (National Research Institute for Food and Nutrition) in Rome, antioxidants protect against cirrhosis of the liver and also prevent gallstones and liver tumours forming. It has been shown that coffee drinking is inversely proportional to the chances of developing a tumour: a person drinking four cups of coffee a day is five times less likely to contract the disease than someone not drinking any at all. A liver in full working order is essential for life and it is uplifting to know that our much-loved cup of coffee can also have a beneficial effect on this organ.

Left: examples of types of food containing natural antioxidants (onions, cauliflowers, broccoli, soya, olive oil and olives, red wine, citrus fruits, green and black tea).

BODY AND BRAIN IN PERFECT SHAPE

How many of us like to show off how well-read we are by relying just on our memories? Who has never had occasion to quote a few lines of poetry learnt at school or recently read?

Well, coffee has a role to play in this mechanism. Memory can be divided into short-term (or working) memory, in other words the system involved in ordering things with which we are currently concerned, and long-term memory, a sort of large, stable warehouse with greater capacity. Caffeine is an aid to short-term memory when it is involved in handling information coming from outside. It produces faster, clearer thought and makes one more alert making learning easier. In other words, coffee optimizes the energy resources we all have and use for learning.

Caffeine helps to revive a tired mind, increasing attentiveness even when there are a thousand things happening that distract us. It is a vital help every time our concentration wavers, for example when revising for an exam. Let's now have a look at how caffeine is involved in improving physical performance. So far, research has shown that drinking coffee reduces fatigue in those who do sport or take physical exercise.

Caffeine is a light stimulant and its effect depends on the activity performed. When the effort is monotonous and it is hard to find the motivation to continue, it can help find the energy to press on and makes us feel less tired when we stop. These effects seem to be more pronounced when exertion is moderate and lasts longer, than with quick spurts of intense exertion. As for the appropriate amount to drink, it would appear that the caffeine content of one cup of coffee is enough to make a noticeable difference.

One piece of news is certainly welcome to all athletes: in 2004 the World Antidoping Agency removed caffeine from the list of banned substances.

So, drinking coffee regularly over a long period and in association with a balanced diet can help keep us fit and mentally alert.

Another of the positive effects of coffee is its capacity to protect against the onset of diabetes. Several studies have highlighted the fact that in the context of an otherwise healthy lifestyle (in which people avoid becoming overweight), regular consumption of coffee can have a positive effect on the prevention of type-two diabetes, which is not caused by a lack of insulin, but by the body's inability to make proper use of the hormone. It is not clear for the moment exactly how coffee acts in this regard, nor which of its components are involved. The whole topic remains a fascinating and promising field of study.

Facing page: an indispensable coffee break during an expedition to the Svalbard Islands, within the Arctic Circle.

DECAFFEINATED COFFEE

We have therefore seen that drunk in moderate amounts and according to individual taste, caffeine is basically full of positive characteristics. But this has not stopped it being unjustly attacked, especially when caffeine-based drink consumption was very high, perhaps when "improperly" used as an additive in many soft drinks. It is not hard to see how a sort of "psychological" trend towards caution among certain consumers might lead them to seek a coffee free of caffeine.

Above: two samples of green coffee (i.e. unroasted beans). Normal on the left, decaffeinated on the right.

Facing page: in decaffeination with solvents, filters are employed in order to re-use the dichloromethane, an organic solvent which evaporates at 40 degrees and leaves no traces on the roasted product.

The decaffeination process was invented by Ludwig Roselius in Germany in around 1905 and is often wrongly thought to eliminate the aroma in coffee.

A coffee's flavour depends on the concentration of aromatic substances that develop during the roasting process, while decaffeination is performed on the raw coffee beans. In any case, caffeine, which is an alkaloid found in all types of green coffee, has no real bearing on the taste or aroma even after roasting. However, there may be a slight loss of aroma or the subtlest change if the process is carried out through the medium of water or with unsuitable solvents.

Whatever system is used, decaffeination is performed before the beans are roasted. It is important to understand that carefully selecting a high quality green coffee will always produce an excellent cup, regardless of the caffeine content. If this cup is indeed decaffeinated, it cannot by law contain more than 0.1% caffeine.

Left: decaffeinated coffee beans being poured into jute sacks.

There are three ways to decaffeinate coffee, based on the extraction of caffeine by means of special solvents that dissolve the alkaloid and bear it away.

Decaffeination with water. The caffeine present in green coffee beans is water-soluble. So this method employs very hot water (at 70-80 degrees centigrade), which removes not only caffeine from the beans, but also some aromatic substances, as well as a certain proportion of sugars and proteins. The caffeine is completely eliminated thanks to activated carbon filters. The resulting solution is free of caffeine and is used to treat a fresh batch of green beans, which are decaffeinated through a process known as diffusion without any loss of aroma or taste. This method lasts about eight hours.

Decaffeination with carbon dioxide. The green coffee beans are sprayed with steam and water until they reach the required humidity (40% max). They are then placed in a special machine, known as an extractor, together with carbon dioxide in a so-called supercritical state, in which it is able to diffuse as a gas and solubilize as a liquid. No other substances are required. Extraction takes place slowly in a controlled environment with pressure kept between 120 and 250 atmospheres. Decaffeination with carbon dioxide is a highly selective extraction process, but the equipment required is very expensive and not yet widely used.

Decaffeination with solvents. Once again, the green coffee beans have to be treated with steam first before being placed in the extractors, where the decaffeination takes place through the action of dichloromethane or ethyl acetate (two organic substances permitted in European law). Further steam treatment removes all residues and, finally, roasting eliminates any remaining traces. It is worth underlining that both compounds are highly volatile and no traces are left either in the green beans or still less in the roasted coffee. Ethyl acetate is an organic solvent with two features that make it hard to ignore: it is highly explosive and has a very strong fruity odour, a hint of which can be tasted in the cup.

There is tasting and tasting

THE ART OF COFFEE TASTING

Why should coffee tasting be considered an art? Every activity human beings undertake can result in colossal mistakes, mediocre outcomes or outstanding successes. Turning a mistake into a possible triumph often depends on the will to try, try and try again, gradually building an expertise through trial and error until perfection is achieved at last.

Professional tasters devotedly apply themselves day after day to this one fundamental activity, honing their senses and attempting to find ways to define any new perceptions.

It is not as easy to become a professional taster as one might think. Everyone acquires certain skills and gradually increases them through what they do most frequently. So beware of anyone claiming to be able to turn you into a perfect taster with a crash course. Getting to know how to appreciate the subtleties of coffee is a slow business and takes application day after day because tasting is a process that involves both our senses and our mind.

The standard a taster achieves is directly proportional to his curiosity, his willingness to put himself to the test and the constant application a novice has to display in order to become ever more expert. But this is not the whole story, because the difference between the amateur taster and his professional counterpart also lies in personal aptitude and is strictly related to the genetic legacy we are born with.

But still, have a go! The more you try, the more satisfaction you will derive from noticing improvements in your ability as a taster.

Facing page: tasting samples of coffee in a Brazilian laboratory.

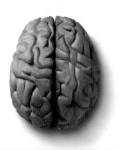

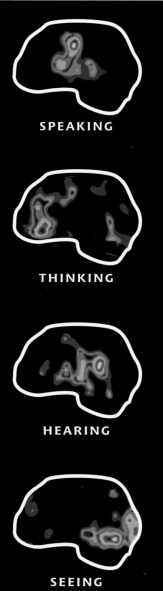

SPEAKING

THINKING

HEARING

SEEING

At this point we shall provide some advice and information which in their simplicity have the great merit of being easy to use even in everyday life and will be a concrete aid in coffee tasting.

The first step is to resist the temptation to add sugar, even if you normally take a spoonful or two. In this way, you will be able to capture the subtle nuances that make, say, a coffee from Colombia different from one from Guatemala.

In order to appreciate the difference, compare the same coffees with and without sugar. Are they still different?

The mental approach to coffee tasting is crucially important. The difference between drinking or tasting a coffee is comparable to that between hearing or listening to a person speak; when tasting or listening, all your attention is focused on capturing and processing information. Similarly, an educated mouth will send stimuli and messages to the brain, where they will be recognised and coded. There is no such thing as a tasting without mental exertion.

Nature has equipped all of us with the necessary instruments to understand and evaluate the characteristics of the food we eat and the beverages we drink, otherwise the human race would not have survived. Imagine what would have happened if our ancestors had not been able to tell the difference thanks to their senses between what was edible and what was poisonous.

But how well trained are our senses?

Not very is the answer. Think for a moment: is it easier to describe a childhood image or the aroma and flavour of something drunk a long time ago? Images certainly do make a stronger impression on our minds, but we can also recall specific tastes and smells.

Our memory can be either voluntary or involuntary. In the former we deliberately recollect something from our past. In contrast, visual, olfactory or tactile impressions can conjure up (in a manner which is not entirely intentional) emotions associated with them in some moment in the past. In this regard, the sense of smell is definitely the one most able to evoke buried memories. Once perceived, odours and smells are correctly recognised. This is where we turn for help to our brain, a wonderful built-in data bank, stocked with information of all kinds linked to situations we have lived through.

Centre, from top to bottom: the areas of the brain involved in speaking, thinking, hearing and seeing.

FLAVOURS AND AROMAS

The tastes found in coffee can be bracketed under acid, bitter and sweet. Unpractised people often put the wrong label on a particular taste and the most common mistakes occur in distinguishing between acidity and bitterness.

First of all, the myth of the tongue being divided into sections needs to be debunked. The various tastes can be detected over all the tongue; sweet flavours can be tasted on the tip, as well as in the middle and on the sides of the tongue, and so on. What does change is the degree to which they are perceived in different points: a solution of water and sugar can be detected at a very low concentration on the tip of the tongue, but it has to be considerably sweeter to be recognised as such on the sides. Generally speaking, if you drink lemon juice you experience a strong physical sensation on the sides of the tongue. This is acidity. Bitterness is perceived to its fullest extent at the back of the tongue. Examples of things eliciting a strong response from this area might be a herbal liqueur, dandelion leaves, or some kinds of medicine.

By paying close attention to the various stimuli you perceive, you will be able to recognise and evaluate the intensity of the various components in the coffee you are tasting.

Assessing aromas is a rather more nuanced business. There are two ways of recognising them: firstly by smelling the coffee (direct or orthonasal perception) and then by concentrating on sensations that appear only after the initial taste (retrolfactory or retronasal perception). It has been proved that we perceive different aromas orthonasally and retronasally and that the same smell is discerned differently.

If the distinction between taste and aroma is still not sufficiently clear, try this small experiment: hold your nose tight with your fingers, taste a little coffee and concentrate on the sensation. This is the taste. Now, without swallowing, release your nose and concentrate on the new messages your brain is receiving. Now you will be able to recognise the aromas. You can try the same trick with other tastes, like fruit juices or sweets. For instance, it is very hard to tell between peach and apricot or tropical fruit, with your nose held shut.

THE FIVE SENSES AT WORK

All five of our senses play their part in savouring a coffee. An awareness of their importance enables us to prepare a coffee properly and to define its characteristics in all their complexity, whichever method we use to make it. Indeed you need a multisensorial approach to tasting, as enjoying a coffee is not just a matter of taste; all our senses are stimulated while we prepare, smell and taste it.

We all recognise the gurgling of a moka, which tells us the coffee is ready. At the same time our sense of sight tells us if the crema on the espresso is up to standard. The sense of smell is obviously paramount in appreciating fragrances and aromas, while the sense of taste tells us how sweet, acid or bitter something is. Finally, the sense of touch allows us to gauge the texture and temperature of food and the density or "body" of a drink. Let us see how best to use our senses to try to capture all the information that a cup of coffee conveys to us and which contribute to making it agreeable or otherwise to drink.

The basic difference between the man in the bar savouring his morning coffee and a true connoisseur or professional taster lies in appreciating the key distinction between "I like it" or "I don't like it" and a well-judged assessment based on objective criteria endorsed and shared by others.

In order to appreciate to the full the subtleties of taste and aroma, our taste buds have to operate under the best conditions possible. This means keeping our mouth a neutral environment by not contaminating it, before a cupping session, with things such as hot, spicy or highly flavoured food, alcohol or smoke.

Rinsing the mouth out with water helps clean the oral cavity before a fresh challenge and is often done between one tasting and another.

Neutral puffed rice can also be used to "clean" the taste buds. Just take a few grains, chew them and pass them over the surface of the tongue. This technique freshens the tongue and sets it up perfectly for the next cupping session.

HEARING, SEEING, SMELLING ESPRESSO

Let's start with the sense of hearing, which is used least in assessing a coffee. Bear in mind though, that trying to make a balanced judgment in a noisy room full of distracting sounds can lead to a swift overload of sensations. And the noises themselves can undermine our concentration, which at this moment should be clearly focused on the contents of the cup.

Sight is our primary sense in apprehending the world and tasting coffee is inevitably affected by its appearance. The crema is what we are really interested in at this stage as it provides essential information on how well the coffee has been made.

As well as introducing the espresso, the crema's job is to retain within the cup all the aromas that would otherwise be released into the air and lost. It thus acts as a sort of protective coating.

The crema's colour ranges from dark brown to light hazel and can even have reddish tones. The so-called *tiger striping*, the dark stripes in the crema created by tiny particles of coffee powder present in the drink, are a sign that the espresso has been perfectly prepared.

Look at the cups on this page and you will be able to tell if your own is as good as it can possibly be.

After a visual assessment of the coffee, we can move on to an olfactory examination to explore the aromas directly released by an espresso.

It is important to stir the coffee with a spoon to "break" the crema and get a clearer impression of the scents drifting up from the liquid. These may be either weak or strong and be described in terms of their elegance and cleanness or, conversely, as being undistinguished and muddy. For instance, in a good quality Arabica one might note caramel, toast and honey tones, as well as hints of citrus fruits and flowers. Some unpleasant smells may be rancid or mouldy or have woody or baggy notes.

Top right and top left, two overextracted espresso coffees; bottom right, underextracted espresso; bottom left, perfect espresso.

A light crema is a sign of an underextracted espresso, which is acid and thin. This is due to the temperature and/or pressure being too low, or to hurried extraction, sometimes as a result of an inadequate quantity of coffee or excessively coarse grinding, causing the cup to fill quickly.

A dark crema with a white patch in the middle is typical of an overextracted coffee, which will have a higher caffeine content and a bitter, astringent taste. In this case the temperature and/or pressure may have been too high, or extraction too protracted, perhaps because too much coffee was used or it was ground too fine, thus inhibiting the flow of coffee.

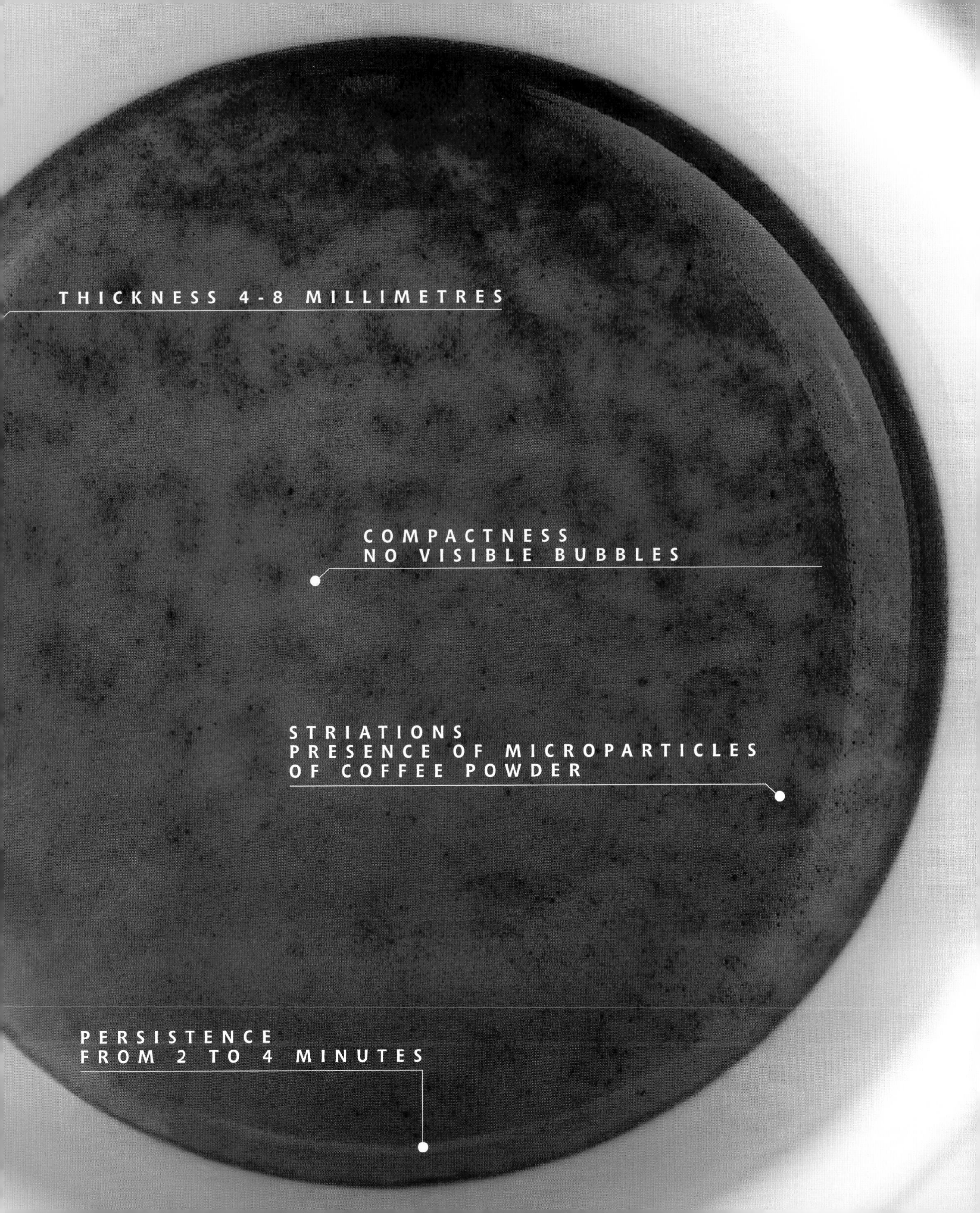

THICKNESS 4-8 MILLIMETRES

COMPACTNESS
NO VISIBLE BUBBLES

STRIATIONS
PRESENCE OF MICROPARTICLES
OF COFFEE POWDER

PERSISTENCE
FROM 2 TO 4 MINUTES

TASTING AN ESPRESSO

Now let's move on to actually tasting the coffee.

Firstly, pay attention to how hot it is. If an espresso coffee is too hot, it might cause more pain than pleasure to the person tasting it.

On the other hand, it is essential that the coffee be drunk immediately. If it is left to cool, the aromas evaporate and the taste loses its fullness and balance.

Professionals use a *goûte café*, a spoon whose head is at right angles to the handle so that the taster can drink the crema and liquid in the correct proportions and at a constant rate. In the absence of a *goûte café*, you can use any mid-sized spoon. Stir your espresso, take a little out with your spoon and sip it.

If you want to improve your responsiveness as a taster, instead of sipping it demurely from your spoon, slurp it noisily, taking in a certain amount of air together with the liquid and creating myriad little bubbles. In this way you produce a sort of aerosol effect, injecting a fine spray of coffee into the mouth. In addition to increasing the coffee-air surface area, you also raise the soft palate, the fibrous muscular tissue on the roof of the mouth separating the oral and nasal cavities. This enables you to perceive the full flavour of the coffee, combining the taste and retronasal experience in one before you swallow it.

Once you have slurped the coffee, keep it in your mouth for a few seconds, to give the taste buds the chance to gauge how sweet, acid and bitter it is.

A good coffee contains a huge array of agreeable aromas, such as caramel (redolent of toffee or fudge), or toastlike (the smell of bread cooking), floral (including jasmine and orange blossom), chocolaty (dark cocoa) and fruity (for example, apricot, melon, and peaches). But there can also be unpleasant notes, which may be present in coffees that have been badly processed or come from diseased plants. It is important to be aware of these too, so that you can distinguish them if you are unlucky enough to encounter them. In these cases experts speak of aromas being woody (the smell of

Above: the *goûte café*, a tasting spoon used by professional tasters, with coffee in it ready to be slurped.

sawdust), jute-like (the smell of coffee sacks), fermented (overripe fruit), rancid (butter that has gone off), earthy (wet soil in a wood), mouldy (smell of damp cellars), barn-like and so on.

Besides covering a variety of tastes and smells, coffee also has its own specific body, which is appreciated through the sense of touch. In order to understand what is meant by the term body in this context, compare water with full cream milk. Water is liquid, while milk feels dense in the mouth. It has body. So it is with coffee. The greater this sense of density, the greater its body. And since the aromas are contained in the oils dissolved in the coffee, a very aromatic coffee will also be particularly thick and velvety.

The term astringent is used to describe the sensation of the mouth feeling dry and the tongue not being able to run freely over the palate, typically experienced when eating unripe fruit or chewing grape seeds. This effect is due to the presence of tannins, substances of vegetable origin, which reduce the lubricating qualities of saliva. These are more commonly found in Robusta coffees, or in Arabica beans that are not sufficiently ripe.

EXAMPLES OF POSITIVE AROMAS

toast-like

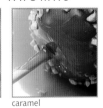
floral

caramel

chocolaty

fruity

EXAMPLES OF NEGATIVE AROMAS

woody

jute

overripe fruit

rancid butter

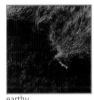
earthy

mouldy

barn-like

ASTRINGENCY

unripe persimmon

raw artichokes

BODY

milk = heavy body

water = thin body

THE AROMAS OF COFFEE

In order to be described as such, a good espresso coffee should satisfy the following requirements: the crema should be compact and hazel coloured and have darker brown stripes (tiger striping), a good balance between acidity and bitterness, a broad range of pleasing aromas, substantial body and a lingering sweet and agreeable *aftertaste*.

It is not easy to find all these features in a single cup of coffee, since every type of coffee has its own distinguishing characteristics, depending on the species (Arabica or Robusta), where it was grown and the processing it underwent.

The characteristics typical of Robusta coffees are a dark crema, sometimes with grey tones, and large bubbles, good body, rather pronounced bitterness, woody or earthy aromas and perceptible astringency.

Turning to the features of good-quality Arabica, it can be said that Ethiopian blends produce a full-bodied, well-balanced coffee with floral, caramel and chocolaty aromas and a compact crema. Central American varieties tend towards a pleasing acidity and clear chocolate and caramel notes. Brazilian coffees are full-bodied with a pleasant toast-like aroma. If you are looking for a coffee with a more emphatic personality, with a pleasurable hint of bitterness, a full body and thick crema, it is best to turn to Indian blends, while a decidedly acid aftertaste with a powerful fruity aroma is what you can expect from coffees from Kenya.

An espresso extracted from Arabica (left) and one extracted from a blend containing Robusta (right).

ETHIOPIA	full-bodied, well-balanced taste, pronounced floral, caramel and chocolaty aromas, with a compact crema
CENTRAL AMERICA	pleasing acidity, with pronounced chocolate and caramel aromas
BRAZIL	full-bodied, with pleasing toast-like and chocolaty aromas
INDIA	punchy, with a pleasurable hint of bitterness, a full body and thick crema
KENYA	decidedly acid aftertaste with a powerful fruity aroma

Each area has its own characteristics and this is no bad thing since everyone has their own personal preference.

The secret of making a top-quality blend lies in finding the right proportions of the very best beans, so that each contributes its own characteristics to the overall flavour without stifling the contribution of the others. Our sense of smell is perfectly adapted to the task of distinguishing the message conveyed by each molecule and combining it with others to provide a fusion of sensations rather than a simple sum.

A TASTER'S CARD

Professional tasters test over a hundred different coffees every day and are able to identify, classify and evaluate the characteristics of each with a precision that enables them to fill out a card containing all their salient features, both positive and negative.

Tasters can employ certain instruments to help them, such as the *goûte café* and taster's cards, which go into great detail and provide the opportunity to assess all of a coffee's characteristics.

But the primary instrument at our disposal remains the human brain, which is called upon to recognize, decipher and quantify the sensations perceived during the few seconds the coffee is in the mouth. As mentioned above, the fullest attention has to be brought to bear on the senses in play: sight in assessing the crema, touch in judging the body and astringency, taste in distinguishing sweet, acid and bitter and smell in picking out the aromas.

A simplified version of one of these cards is printed overleaf so that you can put your own views down in black and white. Use it when comparing different types of coffee; for instance, an Arabica blend as against a Robusta coffee. You could also use it to have a tasting session with friends, giving you the chance to compare notes and see how far opinions can differ.

Of course, it need not be used with just one form of coffee: the card is suitable for all types of preparation, from moka and espresso to filter and so on. Obviously, an analysis of the crema is only possible in the case of espresso coffees.

We advise you to follow the order in the card so that the stages follow one another in a logical sequence, from an examination of the appearance of the beverage to its taste and texture and finally the identification of the aromas present.

If you have the chance, use the card to compare the same coffee prepared in two different ways (say moka and filter). You will soon notice the difference in body, bitterness, acidity, etc. Conversely, try comparing two different coffees prepared the same way and concentrate on the differences you notice. You will find that following the order in the card is a great help.

Above: samples of green, roasted and ground coffee; a graduated beaker to check the volume of the espresso; a coffee made by infusion (left), an espresso (right); a *goûte café* in the middle; a taster's card on the table, ready for the scores to be added for the sample tasted.

COFFEE TASTING CARD

METHOD OF PREPARATION ....

TYPE OF BLEND ....

SIGHT	ONLY FOR ESPRESSO	underextracted	perfect	overextracted
	APPEARANCE OF CREMA	☐	☐	☐

TASTE		under	balanced	over
	ACID	☐	☐	☐
	BITTER	☐	☐	☐
	SWEET	☐	☐	☐

TOUCH		under	balanced	over
	BODY	☐	☐	☐
		present		
	ASTRINGENCY	☐		

SMELL	POSITIVE AROMAS		present	
	CARAMEL		☐	
	CHOCOLATE		☐	
	TOAST		☐	
	FLORAL/FRUITY		☐	
	HONEY		☐	
	NEGATIVE AROMAS	present		
	WOODY	☐		
	MOULD	☐		
	BURNT RUBBER	☐		
	FERMENTED	☐		
	RANCID	☐		

FINAL SCORE   TOTAL POSITIVES ☐   TOTAL NEGATIVES ☐

How we drink it

AROUND THE WORLD IN TEN COFFEES

When in Rome, do as the Romans. There could hardly be a more appropriate saying as far as coffee is concerned. You're unlikely to hear two identical orders while waiting to be served at the bar in a café in Italy. So imagine what can happen if you change country: a different culture inevitably implies different tastes, aromas and experiences.

Right from its infancy, coffee has been served in a variety of different ways and these various methods later spread throughout the world, shedding light on the idiosyncrasies of each. Coffee is deeply ingrained in our way of life: it is not just a drink, but has a profoundly evocative resonance, conjuring up stories of shipping companies and liners, peasants and knowledgeable tasters, daily habits and communal identities. There is a whole ritual to preparing a cup of coffee and it varies according to the local culture, which in Italy's case means that drinking a cup of coffee has acquired an almost sacred status.

The United States are the largest consumers of coffee, accounting for 16% of world production, followed by the chief producer, Brazil, with around 14% (source: International Coffee Organization, June 2012).

But the record for consumption per person, averaging five cups a day, goes surprisingly to northern Europe. Not only is a lot of coffee drunk in Finland, Denmark, Sweden and Luxembourg, but they also pay great attention to the variety of the coffee and where it is grown, with a preference for lightly roasted coffee prepared slowly. Unlike southern European countries, where coffee drinking is mainly an occasion for conviviality and is often drunk at the end of a meal, in Central and Northern Europe it is drunk mostly in the home mid-morning or in the afternoon. The table is laid and coffee is served with little sandwiches, cakes and biscuits.

The young around the world are increasingly drawn to espresso, drunk in a bar or taken as part of an ethnic experience in Italian restaurants.

Something that will perhaps come as a surprise to many is that Italy, the home of the espresso and the country with a bar at every corner is in around tenth place for per capita consumption, but at the same time it is one of the leading exporters of roasted coffee.

Let's find out just where, how and when coffee is drunk around the world.

ISTANBUL

From the days of the Ottoman Empire to the present day, coffee has had a very important part to play in the Turkish lifestyle and in its culture. Coffee drinking and the rituals associated with preparing it have been an integral part of social relations across the centuries, becoming inseparable from the concept of hospitality and even finding a niche in religious and political life.

Coffee reached Istanbul in the mid-sixteenth century thanks to Syrian traders and was soon known as "the milk of chess players and thinkers".

During the next century, coffee was prepared and served at elegant ceremonies held at the magnificent Ottoman court to celebrate betrothals and anniversaries. "Coffee makers" (*kahveci usta*) needed the help of several assistants in preparing coffee for the sultan with the required degree of pomp and show. Young women from the harem were specially trained in the art of making coffee, for their husbands would judge their merits according to the flavour of the black beverage they served them.

Coffee continues to play a very important role in the social and political life of the country to this day. Istanbul has a vast array of delightful cafés and restaurants where friends and families meet to discuss the day's news before a steaming cup of coffee. The great ceremonies have in part been forgotten, but two customs have survived: a bride-to-be still has to serve coffee to her future in-laws (and can conduct herself in such a way as to avoid an unwanted marriage!), and coffee grounds continue to be read to discover the secrets and misdeeds of friends and, above all, rivals.

And what of the future? Well, as they say in Turkey, "drinking a cup of coffee together ensures forty years of friendship". As for the rest, we shall see.

Facing page: people also go to cafés in Turkey to smoke and play cards.

NAPLES

The first "bottega del caffè" opened in Venice in 1645. From that moment the aroma of coffee began to spread the length and breadth of the peninsula. But it was in Naples that it acquired most of its character. In all the world this is the city which is most attached to its *tazzulella*. This is the city of Eduardo De Filippo's theatre, Pino Daniele's songs and the *scugnizzi* (street urchins). It is the city of a thousand faces and colours and as such has much to say about coffee.

At home, coffee is made with a Napolitana stove pot known as a *cuccumella*, which is a sort of coffee pot made up of two metal sections placed one on top of the other, with the topmost having a spout. Between the two is a cylinder for the ground coffee with a basket filter. Using it requires a theatrical sense of gesture: first, the section without a spout is filled with water, the top section is put on and it is put on to boil. When the water is boiling, the gas is turned off and the whole apparatus turned upside down (*a' capo sott*, as the Neapolitans say). After about three minutes the coffee is ready to pour into cups.

What about cafés? For the locals it's like going into a temple (and there is one for every 450 inhabitants). Here an espresso cup holds around 20 millilitres: a really concentrated shot made with a lever-operated espresso machine, with sugar added as the shot is pulled.

VIENNA

The cafés of Vienna are famous throughout the world and they say that drinking a coffee is an Austrian's favourite indoor sport. The fashion for taking a coffee in these surroundings dates from 1683 when the Turks were driven back and had to abandon their hopes of conquering Europe. In their retreat they left behind a large number of sacks containing strange dark beans, which the Viennese had no idea what to do with.

The mystery was solved by George Kolschitzky, a soldier of Polish origin who was familiar with the language and customs of eastern lands. He explained how the Turks used the powder from these crushed

Above: a typical Neapolitan coffee made with a *cuccumella*.
Facing page: a slice of the famously delicious cake served with a cappuccino at the Hotel Sacher in Vienna.

beans to prepare a dark, aromatic beverage which they drank several times a day. Delighted by this news, the citizenry gave Kolschitzky some premises behind St Stephen's Cathedral, which he turned into the first *Kaffeehaus*.

Other European cities had already been captivated by the new drink, but it acquired particular importance in Vienna's social life. Coffee houses sprang up to cater for all classes, where people could go not only to find warmth clasping a hot cup of coffee in their hands, but also to read the newspapers and chat in congenial surroundings about the day's events and political developments.

This is how the art of "wasting time" was born and became part of the natural rhythm of the city without in the least being disturbed by the frenzied pace of modern times. The patrons of the cafés of today still follow their forebears in abiding by an old Viennese saying: "God gave us time, but he said nothing about haste". So it is that the legendary Viennese cafés continue to add their special allure to Vienna's charm.

As for the coffee itself, it was said that a good cup should be "black as night, sweet as love and hot as hell", the way the Arabs like it. Over time the Viennese invented around fifty different ways of making and enjoying a coffee, but always with a slice of cake and a newspaper nearby.

Here is a short list of the most famous coffees in Vienna:

MELANGE	coffee with milk froth
KLEINER BRAUNER	small coffee with milk
GROSSER BRAUNER	large coffee with milk
VERLÄNGESTER	weak coffee similar to American coffee
ESPRESSO	espresso-type coffee
EINSPÄNNER	moka coffee with whipped cream served in a glass
FIAKER	moka coffee laced with cognac, served in a small glass or glass cup

HAMBURG

In Germany, coffee is associated with a state of wellbeing and euphoria, relaxation and fun. This is why it is also often drunk after meals. A typical German morning begins with a steaming cup of coffee and a hearty breakfast.

Coffee continues to be drunk in large quantities throughout the day, whether at work or in leisure hours. People will meet in a *Kaffeehaus*, where they can have a cake with their coffee, or in a *Stehkaffee*, a sort of bar with no tables to sit at, but just a bar at which to stand and order.

Here coffee is traditionally made by filtering it, although in recent times the espresso has been making considerable inroads and milk is gradually taking the place of the ubiquitous cream. The trend is therefore towards a rediscovery of the true aroma of the best quality coffees, prepared with care.

There is a curious thing about the Germans as they rediscover the pleasures of an afternoon ritual. This is the *Kaffeeklatsch*, when friends are invited to a person's home at around five o'clock to socialize. Could this be a new variant of afternoon tea?

AMSTERDAM

On the whole, coffee is drunk in the morning in Holland, at around ten o'clock and in the company of friends. The coffee in question is usually filter coffee, even though an increasing number of people possess an espresso machine at home. The percolators used for filter coffee heat the water until it is hot enough to pour over the coffee in the filter. The number of cups depends on the model of machine used.

Great care is taken over preparing, presenting and serving the coffee. *Koffie verkeed* is the typical Dutch coffee, served with milk in large mugs and often taken with cakes and biscuits, such as the traditional apple tart.

The fact that drinking coffee is part of the process of socializing in welcoming surroundings is very important in Holland. Espresso coffee is regarded as the ideal after-dinner drink and an espresso machine in the home, together with all the accessories, has almost become a status symbol.

OSLO AND STOCKHOLM

In Norway they drink what is commonly regarded as proper coffee: dark and without milk or sugar. Filter coffee has taken its place alongside the traditional form prepared in a metal jug. And as is happening in most other countries, coffee is being increasingly drunk in cafés and bars, where unfamiliar types of coffee, such as the espresso and cappuccino are being introduced.

One of the more curious episodes in the history of coffee occurred in just this part of the world, in eighteenth-century Sweden. Feelings ran high when ranks began to swell in two bitterly opposed factions: one in favour of tea, the other preferring coffee. Tempers became so incandescent that King Gustav III decided to carry out an experiment to prove once and for all which of the two was the better drink. The royal dungeons were said to contain a pair of twins and the king ordered one to drink tea all his life and the other only coffee. The funny thing was that all those involved in the experiment – the king, the doctors and their assistants – died before either of the twins. For the record, the twin forced to drink tea died first, at around 83 years of age. His brother lived to be a hundred, thus achieving coffee's wholly symbolic victory over tea.

Facing page: in some coffee shops in Denmark you can buy roasted coffee beans and have them ground on the spot in big grinders that look as if they have come from the Middle East.

Right: making a filter coffee. Boiling water works its way through coffee powder contained in a paper filter.

PARIS

Paris, toujours l'amour: this truly is the city where a love of coffee is born at breakfast time. Filter coffee is the favourite way to accompany a French breakfast with a croissant or a baguette. Another cup, without milk, is drunk after lunch. Then there are the *brûleries*, where the head-spinning choice of blends of varying intensity and pungency attract coffee lovers like magnets. Between the seventeenth and nineteenth centuries any intellectual worth his salt would make straight for the *Paris café* in vogue at the time. Voltaire, for example, seems to have had a passion for a mixture of coffee and chocolate, while Honoré de Balzac claimed in his *Treatise on Modern Stimulants*, published in 1838, that coffee invigorates the brain and gives rise to creative ideas and brilliant thoughts. Espresso coffee is popular in bars and restaurants, especially in the north, where it is taken rather longer than in Italy.

LONDON

There's no doubt about it: the only reason the English drink even the little coffee they do is so they can be more alert and have more energy. To make sure they get a decent cup, coffee lovers often have to go to the office with a thermos of their own blend. Weekends offer a little more time to experiment with something a little different and the little coffee cups come out of the sideboard – not to be sipped from slowly and meditatively, but as symbols of a dynamic, carefree, fast-paced way of life. When all's said and done though, while it is true that there has been an increase in coffee consumption, tea remains the national drink par excellence.

NEW YORK

The first coffee of the morning is the classic filter coffee we have all seen in American TV series. The coffee can also be made in a percolator and drunk from *mugs* accompanied perhaps by a muffin. Businessmen are often seen dodging through the traffic in the streets downtown clutching their morning dose of hot coffee in big paper cups. In New York, and in the States in general, coffee consumption reflects the American temperament: anything goes; this is the place to explore the potential of single plantation coffees, organic coffees and unusual aromas. There is no real custom of drinking coffee after meals, although it is certainly more common at weekends.

TOKYO

Snubbing the strictures of the ancient oriental philosophers, which set such great store by calmness and meditation, people rush around so much in Tokyo that they don't have any time for themselves. All this is reflected in the coffee, which tends to be instant. In Japanese culture, coffee is generally regarded as an energizing beverage. Cans or little plastic bottles containing a range of cold coffees can be bought in bars or from the ubiquitous vending machines. Japan is one of the largest consumers of this type of coffee in the world. European-style restaurants and chains of *coffee shops* only began to appear in any numbers from around the year 2000.

Facing page: a shaken iced coffee, served with a sprinkling of cocoa powder.

OPPORTUNITY MAKES THE COFFEE

Drinking a coffee is now an everyday activity and certainly one of the small pleasures of life –- when you get up in the morning, for breakfast, after a morning's work or at the end of a good meal. There's always room for a coffee!

Of course very few realize that drinking or serving a coffee is associated with a series of small rules and rites which have become part of "coffee etiquette", which is all that remains of the ceremony of the past when every gesture was important and had to be performed just so.

These conventions are now more relaxed, but it is still eye-opening to know how our daily cuppa ought to be served and drunk.

If you are entertaining guests, the coffee should on no account be served in the kitchen but on an occasional table accompanied by a slice of cake or perhaps some biscuits.

If things are to be done in style, a porcelain service should be used with a cup, a saucer and a small plate presented on an elegant tray.

Always ask your guest if he takes sugar with his coffee and if so how much, naturally without adding any remarks regarding his tastes.

If sugar is added, the coffee should be stirred lightly from the top downwards. The cup is raised to the lips in the right hand, while the left holds the saucer.

As for the correct quantity of coffee, etiquette suggests the preheated cups should be two thirds full.

The choice of spoons is another important matter. These should always be coffee spoons and not tea spoons, which are a little larger.

On the following pages are some tips on how to delight your guests by making the perfect coffee using a variety of the most widespread methods.

TURKISH COFFEE

In order to make a perfect Turkish coffee you need to use very finely ground coffee. Traditional grinders used to be made of brass, which produced a coffee so fine as to be almost powder, like icing sugar. Obviously you can now use an electric grinder.

Turkish coffee has to be made in a *cezve*, a special type of cone-shaped, long-handled jug made of copper or brass, whose bottom section is wider than the top.

There are a number of steps in the process:
1. Pour the water into the *cezve* (around 50 millilitres per cup).
2. Add sugar to taste and stir until dissolved. In many countries Turkish coffee is flavoured with spices, such as cardamom and cinnamon. If you would like to experiment, try adding the spices finely ground.
3. Bring to the boil, then remove the *cezve* from the flame and add a spoonful of coffee per person plus one "for the pot".
4. The coffee should then be boiled twice, taking care to remove the *cezve* from the source of heat between one boiling and the next and skimming off the crema that forms and stirring well.
5. Add a spoonful of cold water before serving so as to ensure all the coffee powder sinks to the bottom and pour into the cups without filtering.

NEAPOLITAN COFFEE

Neapolitan coffee achieves a fine balance between a light body and a full flavour.

The steps for using a Napoletana pot:
1. Put 5-6 grams of medium-ground coffee per cup in the filter in the middle section of the percolator.
2. Add water to the bottom section.
3. Close the percolator and bring the water to the boil.
4. When it is boiling, remove it from the heat source and turn it upside down so that the water passes through the filter into what is now the warm but empty bottom section.
5. Wash the percolator in water and a delicate washing-up liquid and dry thoroughly.

MOKA COFFEE

The Moka pot spread throughout Europe in the 1930s because it is easy to use and produces quite a full-bodied coffee with plenty of aroma. The unmistakeable hourglass design is the classic moka, but there are many other types and shapes on the market. Whatever the design, all mokas work on the principle of steam building up in the base until the pressure (around one atmosphere) forces the water through the ground coffee in the filter.

Here are some tips on how to obtain a perfect moka coffee.
1. Fill the base with cold water up to the level of the valve, sometimes marked within. It is essential to use the right amount of water so that the coffee has the right body (neither too heavy nor too thin) and to avoid calcium deposits on the valve itself.
2. Put the coffee in the filter in an even layer, patting it down lightly if necessary. Don't press down too hard and avoiding forming "mounds". The water has to be able to pass through the whole cake of coffee uniformly.

3. Ensure that the filter disk and rubber gasket are in place. Screw the two sections of the moka together tightly.

4. Put the moka on a low flame. The coffee will begin to fill the top section. Take the moka off the fire before the machine starts to gurgle. The most complex aromas are released at around 60 degrees, the temperature of the first coffee to enter the top section. If you wait for the gurgling to start, the last drops of coffee will be burnt and risk making the whole cup taste bitter.

5. Rinse the moka out with water after every use, if necessary adding a few drops of a mild washing-up liquid, and dry thoroughly to avoid a build-up of calcium deposits.

FILTER COFFEE

If prepared with the right equipment, filter coffee is full-flavoured and aromatic. It is important to grind the beans to the correct consistency, because when the coffee is not ground finely enough it is too weak in the cup and if it is too fine the result is a bitter drink. In the case of filter coffee, medium-ground beans are ideal.

Filter coffee is best made as follows.
1. First of all, heat the carafe for a few minutes by filling with hot water.
2. Put a heaped spoonful (7-8 grams) of coffee for every two cups of coffee, each holding 100-150 millilitres. You can always change the proportions according to taste.
3. Boil the correct amount of water and pour over the grounds. Use a thermos flask to keep the coffee hot and fla-voursome and drink within two hours. Glass pots connected directly to a heat source should be avoided because they risk boiling your coffee and making it taste burnt and bitter.
4. Clean the apparatus regularly, preferably on a weekly basis, to remove any coffee residues and any calcium de-posits, which could spoil the taste of the coffee. Special products for cleaning these devices and keeping them in perfect condition are available on the market.

MELIOR SYSTEM

Coffee made with the Melior method employs a cylindrical pot equipped with a plunger which is pres-sed down on a mixture of hot water and coffee powder, separating the drink from the grounds. The secret of preparing a perfect cup – with a minimum of suspended particles – is to grind the coffee to the right uniform, consistent texture, which should be fine enough to give a full, rich, aromatic flavour, but not so fine as not to be separated from the water. Should the coffee appear murky, you can grind it less finely. Moreover, if the coffee is too fine, it can block the filter and make it hard to press the plunger down the length of the cylinder.

The coffee is prepared thus.
1. Place the pot on a dry, flat, non-slip surface. Hold the handle firmly and remove the plunger.
2. Add a heaped spoonful of coffee (7-8 grams) for every 200 millilitres of water.
3. Pour the hot (not boiling) water into the pot.
4. Reposition the plunger and press down slowly and evenly. This will give a better coffee and avoid it squirting out.
5. Rinse the pot out with water and a little mild washing-up liquid after each use and dry thoroughly.

ESPRESSO COFFEE

Perhaps the quintessential coffee. An espresso has all the characteristics of a solution, because it contains a combination of different ingredients (acids, proteins and sugars). But it is also an emulsion, since it contains oils that convey its aromas and give the coffee body. During extraction (as the process is known) a small proportion of these oils (around 0.1%) is absorbed by the liquid as a result of the pressure, lending it the viscosity that gives the coffee its pleasant aftertaste, lingering in the mouth long after the coffee itself has been swallowed. And then again an espresso is also a suspension in which tiny particles of coffee powder and minute gas bubbles are dispersed in the liquid.

Making a perfect espresso is not as simple as it might appear, especially from the technical point of view. In order to enjoy an excellent cup of coffee in your own home it is important to use single doses of coffee. The idea in developing this system was to enable everyone to make a coffee of consistently high quality, regardless of one's experience.

Single dose coffees are simply ready-prepared single portions of roasted, tamped and ground coffee that ensure that all the rules for making a perfect espresso are followed when used in the appropriate machine: an ideal quantity of coffee (7 grams); the right pressure in the machine (between 15 and 18 atmospheres) and an ideal water temperature (between 90 and 93 degrees) and coffee temperature (between 78 and 82 degrees).

The coffee capsules can be made of a special paper (coffee pods) or other materials.

Counter-top espresso machines and single-dose capsules or pods together form a complete system. These systems can be *"open"* or *"closed"*. An open system is one in which a given pod can be used with different types and makes of machine. A closed system is one where the particular espresso machine model has a dedicated pod specially designed to fit into it.

These machines are very easy to use. All you have to do is place a capsule or pod in the filter holder and switch the machine on. The extraction takes thirty seconds and provides the correct volume of coffee in a cup (25-30 millilitres). To drink it at its best, we recommend that the cup be warmed first, thus preventing the coffee from cooling too quickly. If the machine does not have a cup warming function, you can use boiling water, if necessary taking it from the machine itself before making the coffee.

THE WORLD IN A COFFEE BEAN

Coffee lands

Coffee is cultivated in many different areas and in a variety of climates, although always in countries in the tropical belt of the planet. Numerous factors therefore affect a coffee plant's growth: latitude, altitude, temperature, rainfall, the amount of sunlight, the nature of the soil and of course the method of cultivation. Coffee grows on the sides of volcanoes in Guatemala and in the great red plains of Brazil, it clambers up the narrow terraces of mountains in Yemen and spreads through the exuberant forests of Ethiopia. Further west, it is at home in the humid valleys of Cameroon, while to the east it has adapted to the monsoon mountain chains of India.

Coffee cultivation is extremely varied throughout the world and even in a single country a variety of different methods can co-exist, chosen by farmers according to the characteristics of the land or the morphology of the terrain.

Coffee is grown in around sixty countries and most of the plantations belong to small landowners. Medium sized and large estates can be found in Colombia, India, Guatemala, Indonesia, Vietnam, Kenya and Ivory Coast. Supply is very diversified: ranging from farmers working small or extremely small holdings (sometimes even under a hectare) and selling their crop to local exporters (often with cooperatives as middle men), to big landowners operating on an industrial scale. Brazil, with its estates covering thousands of hectares, is a case apart and cannot be compared with other producers.

Besides the division into large and small landowners, entailing a different economic approach to cultivation, a second discriminating factor is whether cultivation is in the shade or in full sunshine, on hillsides or in mountain forests, in the plain or on terraces.

Plantations in the shade are associated with plants other than coffee (spices, bananas, fruit), which provide improved microclimates and mitigate the effects of the wind and sudden temperature changes

Facing page: In the Yirga Cheffe region of Ethiopia, coffee is left to dry in the sun on mats laid out in the courtyards of the small farmers' houses.

and help to reduce soil erosion. This type of cultivation is usually carried out by small landowners and obviously entails inferior profitability per hectare.

Cultivation in full sunlight is carried out by large landowners who are keen to automate each stage in the processing as far as possible. Intensive cultivation requires a greater irrigation of the soil, which gradually has the nutrients leached out of it, in turn meaning the farmers have to employ industrial fertilisers. However, all this extra expense does lead to large yields and ensures greater profitability per hectare.

Economic dependence on coffee is especially evident in Africa, where the proportion of coffee in overall exports comfortably exceeds 60%. These coffee-based economies which are common in Africa (in Ethiopia and Kenya, for example), but are also present in Central America (for instance, in Colombia), are counterbalanced by the situation in Brazil, which has managed to reduce its dependence on coffee as a cash crop over the past few years. By the second half of the 1970s coffee accounted for 20% of Brazil's exports. Thanks to increased diversification in products aimed at the export market and accelerated industrial development, this figure has dropped to around 3-4%. Even so, Brazil remains the largest producer of coffee in the world, and also the first producer of Arabica coffee; accounting for over a third of world production: 2.2 million hectares under coffee, 5 million employed and 300,000 producers, 43 million sacks a year (32-33 million of Arabica coffee, 10-11 million of Robusta coffee). Colombia is the second producer of Arabica coffee in this table, with 6% of world production and almost 8 million sacks a year.

In spite of all these differences, there is one thing that remains unchanging: it is certain that coffees grown in a given country, and even a particular area, will always have their own unmistakeable characteristics setting them apart from the others. In this sense coffee can be compared to wine, except that in coffee's case the influence of the "terroir" is if anything even more marked.

Arabica coffees are generally speaking always notably aromatic, subtle and smooth. Robusta coffees tend to be more bitter and woody.

Guatemalan Arabica, for instance, represents only about 3% of total world production, but the quality is superb, making an extremely sweet coffee with medium acidity, an intense, flowery aroma and a

taste with chocolaty undertones. It is the ideal bean to add character to espresso blends and is also a common component in filter coffees.

African countries only produce a limited amount of Arabica, but the quality is excellent. Kenya's unfluctuating

SOUTH AMERICA	45 %
CENTRAL AMERICA	14 %
AFRICA	13 %
ASIA AND OCEANIA	28 %

Percentage of world coffee production (source: International Coffee Organization, June 2012).

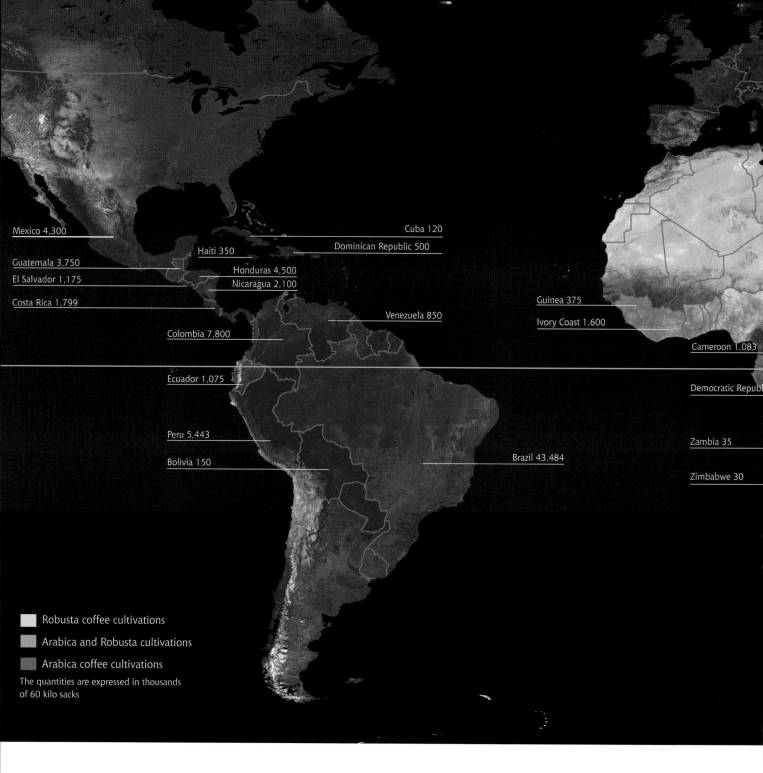

Mexico 4,300

Cuba 120

Dominican Republic 500

Haiti 350

Guatemala 3,750

El Salvador 1,175

Honduras 4,500

Nicaragua 2,100

Costa Rica 1,799

Guinea 375

Venezuela 850

Ivory Coast 1,600

Colombia 7,800

Cameroon 1,083

Ecuador 1,075

Democratic Republ

Peru 5,443

Zambia 35

Bolivia 150

Brazil 43,484

Zimbabwe 30

Robusta coffee cultivations

Arabica and Robusta cultivations

Arabica coffee cultivations

The quantities are expressed in thousands of 60 kilo sacks

The main coffee-producing countries. Brazil is the leading producer with around 43 million sacks. Vietnam is the leading producer of Robusta coffee with 20 million sacks (source: International Coffee Organization, June 2012).

temperate climate provides an acidic, aromatic coffee which is ideal for filter coffee, while Ethiopia produces one of the most highly sought-after Arabica beans, with a conspicuously flowery nose and caramel notes in the taste.

A full body and an agreeable hint of bitterness and spicy aroma are the strong points of an Indian coffee.

The coffees of El Salvador, Costa Rica, Mexico, Panama and Honduras are sweet, with a

India 5,333

Thailand 693

Vietnam 20,000

Philippines 300

Ethiopia 6,500

Uganda 3,212

Kenya 680

Rwanda 400
Burundi 250

Indonesia 8,250

Tanzania 534

Papua New Guinea 1,415

Madagascar 650

welcome hint of acidity. A feature shared by all Central American coffees is their sweetness and lightness.

Brazilian beans often act as the basic framework around which blends are built, while Colombian beans are used to lend the blend the right degree of sweetness.

Asia and West Africa (Ivory Coast, and Cameroon) concentrate on the Robusta variety, while the chief producers are Vietnam (20 million sacks per year) and Indonesia (more than 8 million sacks per year), as compared with Brazil's 10-11 million sacks.

Ethiopia

FULL NAME	Yeltyop'iya Fēdēralawi Dēmokrasīyawī Rīpeblīk (Federal Democratic Republic of Ethiopia)
CAPITAL	Addis Ababa (2,979,086 inhabitants)
OFFICIAL LANGUAGE	Amharic and Tigrinya
GOVERNMENT	federal republic
INDEPENDENCE	1941
SURFACE	1,127,127 km²
POPULATION	82,101,998 (2011 estimate)
DENSITY	73 inhabitants per km²
COFFEE PRODUCTION	6,500,000 (60-kilo sacks)
GDP	29,717 million US dollars
CURRENCY	Ethiopian Birr

Sources: *Calendario Atlante De Agostini*, 2012; International Coffee Organization, June 2012

Facing page: an aerial view of the small plots of coffee in the Ethiopian Coffee Forest plateau in the Yuya region.

Below: offering guests a coffee is an ancient custom in Ethiopia which is still widely practised in the original manner and slow rhythm.

ETHIOPIA: THE GREAT BLACK MOTHER

Ethiopia is a land of astonishing beauty and was the first African country to gain independence.

Few countries in the world can boast as many legends and fascinating attractions as Ethiopia. As big as Italy, France, Switzerland, Austria and Belgium put together, it covers much of the Horn of Africa (the easternmost corner of the continent). It lies between the Red Sea and the Indian Ocean, but has no coastline, bounded as it is by Eritrea, Kenya, Djibouti, Somalia and Sudan. It is a land of high, snow-capped mountains, rising to over four thousand metres, as well as torrid plains, dropping even to below sea level.

The scenery is always powerful and peppered with awe-inspiring gorges, sharp peaks, bottomless chasms and rocky outcrops.

Among the more unusual mountain landscapes are the so-called *Ambe mountains*, whose cone-like peaks are flat, as if neatly chopped off with a knife. Volcanoes and lakes are sprinkled down the Great Rift Valley running from north-eastern Ethiopia all the way to Mozambique. Some believe Ethiopia to be the cradle of mankind and a number of hominid fossils dating to over three million years ago have been discovered in the Awash Valley. The most famous Australopithecine of all, Lucy, was found in 1974 and is considered our earliest forebear.

Ethiopia also happens to be the native land of coffee. As legend has it, it was here that the first plant was noticed, when the shepherd Kaldi's sheep wandered off one night and returned the next morning full of energy after gorging on the plant's luscious red berries. Ethiopia is a land full of charms yet to be discovered, inhabited by people with a ready smile. Crossing it is a bit like taking a journey back to the origins of man. All the stages in our evolution, otherwise only read about in history books, can be encountered here. Time has stood still and people lead untroubled lives, in spite of the fact that things are not easy from an economic standpoint. Gone are the glories of the past and Ethiopia now has one of the lowest GDPs per head in the world.

What immediately strikes the visitor is the enormous number of people on the move in Ethiopia, perhaps without even a clear destination in mind. Some run, dressed in their Sunday best with jacket and tie, walking stick in hand. They bound along in the stifling heat in the middle of the road. Ethiopians know that others have a higher standard of living, but one of their great virtues and extraordinary strengths is their willingness to make do.

Frenzy reigns supreme in the capital, Addis Ababa. An unbearable smog blankets the city, making the air unbreathable and colours are pale and washed out. Cars hurtle to their unlikely destinations leaving clouds of black smoke in their wake. The whole city looks like a building site, with new constructions going up, down or being repaired – always using the most basic technology, consisting of wheelbarrows and pulleys.

Driving out into the countryside beyond the city is a little like watching an endless film about the "comedy of mankind". If you look carefully, you can find all aspects of human behaviour. There's just one long, grey, sharp, throbbing and vibrant road, built by the Chinese at the end of the 1990s. This is the one and only road in this land of red soil and it leads straight to Kenya. The landscape changes suddenly along this long strip of concrete, as if it marked a boundary. As you leave the city behind and begin to approach the country the

Below: children selling local products to passers-by on a road in Ethiopia; in this case green coffee and pineapple.

Facing page: Ethiopians are a people on the move; they generally travel on foot down the country's main road.

After picking in the Ethiopian plantations, the sacks full of cherries are left by the sides of the roads to wait for the lorries to take them to the processing centres.

Facing page: fragrant white coffee blossom.

colours and faces change and even the quality of the light alters. You lose all sense of distance and time as everything dissolves in the general chaos and improvisation, which nonetheless seems miraculously to work. This is a fairytale world where the scenery is so beautiful that it brings tears to your eyes, but the spell is broken as soon as your gaze meets that of one of the locals. These are no cartoon yokels placed here to excite pity or commiseration, but real people inviting you to become a part of their lives and asking to be understood.

All Ethiopians want is to get through the day, work and have fun. And they really do work without a pause, whether in sun or rain. Barefoot, they trudge down kilometres of dirt road with protruding stones without batting an eye. The hours pass and their meagre pay is mainly spent in small markets where they buy fresh meat and various plastic goods, possibly a drink, clothes and imported Chinese shoes.

Ethiopians don't save: many families don't even manage to get through the slow seasons when work is hard to come by and there is not enough work in the fields to go round. Fortunately, the World Bank or some aid organization steps in with emergency funds.

THE ORIGINS OF MAN AND ARABICA

Ethiopia is rightly considered the cradle of Arabica, but, incredibly, coffee production only accounts for 2-3% of GDP. It is easy to see why: 35 million hectares are suitable for coffee growing, but in fact a little under 400,000 are farmed (source: FAO). The government is trying to reduce its country's economic dependence on coffee and to boost the cultivation of other crops with a higher yield that can be harvested throughout the year. But this policy will take time to bear fruit and for the moment coffee is set to be the most important crop.

The *Typica* variety of *Coffea arabica* is native to Ethiopia. In 1994 the Ethiopian government commissioned a German team to seek a specific native variety which could legitimately be called a real Ethiopian coffee plant, and in 2002 they finally succeeded. It is called *Geisha*, from the name of a forest south-west of Addis Ababa.

Coffee can be said to grow throughout Ethiopia, except in the region of Harrar, in the north, and to the east of Addis Ababa, where the land is too dry. Most plantations lie in the south of the country, in the Sidamo and Yirga regions. The conditions in this area are ideal for the coffee plant: temperatures of around 27-28 degrees centigrade, an altitude of between 1200 and 1900 metres and a reasonably long rainy season, which begins in April and continues until October.

In eastern Ethiopia, coffee grows at an altitude of 1500 to 1800 metres. Coffees grown here are known as *Longberry Harrar* (large cherries), *Shortberry Harrar* (small cherries) and *Mocha Harrar* (typically consisting of *peaberries*, fruit with only one seed instead of two).

Ethiopian coffees are renowned for their acidity, chocolate aroma and intense, fruity undertones redolent of the countryside where they were grown. *Harrar* is notably sweet, with a full body and pronounced acidity. Eastern Ethiopia

also produces a washed coffee called *Ghimbi*, which has a similar taste to *Harrar* but tends to be richer, more balanced and more full-bodied.

Southern Ethiopia produces a washed coffee with an acid taste and powerful aroma. These coffees are known by the name of the district where they are grown (such as Sidamo), or by more evocative names like *Ethiopian Fancies*, or *Ethiopian Estate Grown*. The best known is *Yirga Cheffe*, which has an unrivalled aroma and taste, a bright, elegant body and explosive flavour.

Above: in the Yirga Cheffe region of Ethiopia, coffee plants can sprout spontaneously thanks to the indigestible seeds dispersed by birds in their droppings.

Facing page: a forest plantation; coffee plants grow and produce fruit sheltered by tall trees.

THE COFFEE FORESTS

Even today it is moving to find tiny shoots breaking through the untended, hostile soil of the forest, with its huge variety of plants carpeting the land: lush shrubs coated with butterflies, coffee plants and other vegetation form a green curtain and in the play of light and shade a seemingly infinite number of trees form a luxuriant canopy.

Coffee growing in Ethiopia is as close to spontaneous as can be.

Small farmers account for fully 96% of the coffee grown and many work less than a hectare. Plots are often rented from the state on very long leases (30-50 years).

The remaining 4% is in the hands of large nationalized companies. Ethiopians sow coffee seeds by placing them directly in a hole in the ground where the plants are then to grow (pit sowing). This is a very basic farming technique. Certain general procedures are of course still carried out, such as the addition of organic fertilizer and regular pruning to "invigorate" the plants and encourage them to produce fresh growth.

There are no artificial systems of irrigation and cultivation continues in the most natural manner possible. The plants spontaneously produce fresh growth in their natural habitat and can be successfully transplanted to other areas with a minimum of fuss and only minor human involvement.

A family of Ethiopian farmers in the Yirga Cheffe region has just brought its crop to the washing station to have it assessed and to sell it.

PICKING AND PROCESSING

In Ethiopia, the fifth largest producer of coffee in the world with almost 5% of the total, 12 million people are employed in coffee growing and processing.

Coffee is their *cash crop*: it is grown not for local consumption but for sale in the market. Since cultivators reach the harvesting season after a period when income is scarce, the fact they at last have coffee to sell means they once again have a sure revenue.

Traditionally, only part of the coffee crop is sold as cherries, the rest is dried and stored by the farmer, who uses it as unofficial currency in exchange for other goods. Over the past few years the price of coffee has increased regularly and producers are now tempted to sell more and more of their fruit.

This has reduced the amount of stored dry coffee. But since Ethiopian farmers are not used to saving earnings as such, the lack of "money" for use in barter means they live in perennial poverty, especially during the months prior to harvesting.

The crop is picked at different times depending on the area, but generally speaking picking begins in October-November and finishes in January-February. Harvesting is performed by hand and even transport is labour intensive, the farmers carrying the bags themselves, sometimes aided by mules.

They can be seen walking all alone down long, winding roads lost in their thoughts and fully aware of their role as "gold bearers". Others prefer to have someone to chat to and are accompanied by men of all ages on their trudge of several kilometres between the fields and the washing centres.

A coffee bean's day in Ethiopia is a long and tiring one. The day begins at dawn, when the farmers set off to their fields on foot. Some are lucky enough to live close to their crop, others have miles of dusty road to trudge along. The whole family, from grandparents to their young grandchildren help in selecting the cherries to be picked.

At the start of the season no distinctions are made: they pick everything, glowing red or raw green. The dearth of work over the previous months turns the first days of the harvest into a real festival. Even when they exist, the roads are pot-holed and hard to negotiate. Particoloured family members stand out against the bright green of the vegetation, each with his own job to do, each carrying a tool in the bustling throng. Then there are those who decide they are just too exhausted and lie down in the middle of the road for a nap. But the day slips by quickly and there's no time to lose. When the harvesting is at its height no one sleeps very long. Once they have been filled with cherries, the jute sacks are carried in wheelbarrows or on muleback to the collection points where the coffee is processed.

Above: a sack of coffee ready for sale, carefully stored in the head of the family's room (Yirga Cheffe, Ethiopia).

Below: picking out faulty beans (Yirga Cheffe, Ethiopia).

At a washing station. After fermentation, the coffee is washed in troughs with running water.

Facing page, above: sorting the good from the spoilt cherries; below: the washed beans are spread on wooden stretchers and carried to the drying areas (Yirga Cheffe, Ethiopia).

Scattered throughout the forest in the middle of nowhere, these areas stand out like oases where the pickers can gratefully unload their precious burdens. It's like watching the Three Kings arriving at the manger, except that there are a lot more than three and their hands bear the signs of the day's labours, caked as they are with resin and the sweetish juice of the cherries.

The sacks may also be bought along the way by middlemen, known as *akrabi*, who use all their bargaining skills to beat the price down to what they are prepared to pay on the spot. There may sometimes be a second middleman with his own vehicle, which he uses to take the cherries directly to the washing stations.

Quality control obviously takes a back seat in all this haggling, which is why careful monitoring is required from when the first coffee beans reach the washing points right up until they are stored in the ships that are to take them to Europe. But this is both a time-consuming and costly process, requiring patience, experience and above all a lot of enthusiasm.

At all events, Ethiopian coffee is a top quality product in itself. But there are those who are not happy to take the coffee's origin as a guarantee of quality and insist on checking the whole green coffee supply chain.

The starting point in ensuring the quality of the finished product is to buy the cherries directly and exclusively from the producer, so that the ripeness can be checked in loco. Therefore the first selection is carried out at the moment of purchase. The sack, sometimes containing only a few kilos of cherries, is emptied out onto a sort of big tray like a bed to be checked by the first sorters.

Below: the coffee is dried in drying "beds". The women constantly stir the beans singing to the rhythm of the drums. The stirring prevents moulds forming and ensures the beans dry evenly. Any remaining flawed beans are tossed out.

Facing page: a view of the drying area, where corrugated iron panels are used to protect the beans from too much sun.

The berries then undergo a second inspection, before being put back into the sacks and into the long queue waiting to be weighed.

Once weighed, the cherries are poured into a kind of large trench and flowing water carries them to the depulper, which removes the pulp and skin from around the coffee beans. The beans are then left to ferment in large concrete tanks (3 metres by 6) and in one or two days (depending on the temperature and humidity of the air) they acquire the acidity typical of Ethiopian coffee.

The fermented coffee is then put into troughs and washed in running water with the aid of special brooms, often to the rhythm of music.

At the end of this process, the coffee beans are fed through hand-operated spouts into wooden stretchers with a metal mesh. When full, these are carried off by two men to the drying area, where

the coffee is carefully arranged on wooden trestles supporting a metal framework, on which is laid a jute cloth.

The most remarkable sight is the crowd of people (mostly women) who spend the day looking after their precious beans. Dozens of brightly-coloured figures delicately stir the expanse of coffee beans, removing any foreign matters and ensuring the drying process is uniform. In the evening the whole apparatus is covered with large jute and nylon awnings as protection against any rain. Women perform all these tasks to the rhythm of *bongo* drums, played by the same people who act as quality controllers. The music makes the work less monotonous and gives shape to the day.

Below: in Ethiopia, the washed coffee beans are sometimes dried in front of the farmers' dwellings. Quality control is virtually impossible when this traditional method is used, since birds and other animals can walk across the mats freely.

Facing page: drying beds (Edido, Ethiopia).

The cherries can be dried on mats in front of the house in the Ethiopian Coffee Forest.

THE COFFEE RITUAL

The coffee ritual is a real art form in Ethiopia, evolving into a kind of entertainment and an opportunity to keep in touch with friends. Unlike what is customary on our continent, making and carefully sipping a coffee can take almost half a day: three hours of socializing, mostly organized by old women for members of their family and neighbours. This gives us an insight into how important this beverage is in the daily life of this country. According to tradition, freshly-cut grass has to be laid on the ground, then a small coal-fired stove is lit and some recently washed green coffee beans are roasted on it. The hovering gestures of the women's hands as they gently roast the beans are as graceful as can be. The smell of the roasting beans blends with the tang of incense in the bare room, enveloping all present in a fairy tale world.

In Ethiopian villages, the coffee ceremony is a time for people to meet and socialize.

When the roasting is complete, the guests are invited to appreciate the richness of the aroma and, with their consent, the coffee beans are put in the grinder. The ground coffee is then put in an earthenware jug full of boiling water. A few minutes later the coffee is ready, strong, dark and fruity, with a slightly smoked aftertaste. It is often flavoured with local herbs.

Sitting in a *bunna-bet* (*bunna* in Amharic means coffee, while *bet* means house) with friends is an unforgettable experience. There is a great hubbub as people chat and sew, guests are blessed and evil spirits are expelled from the house.

Traditionally, only one or three cups of coffee can be drunk, never two. Patience and the slow passing of time are once again central to the occasion.

India

FULL NAME	Republic of India – Bhārat Juktarashtra
CAPITAL	New Delhi (294,783 inhabitants)
OFFICIAL LANGUAGE	English, Hindi and 21 other minor languages
GOVERNMENT	federal republic
INDEPENDENCE	1947
SURFACE	3,287,263 km²
POPULATION	1,210,193,422 (2011 census)
DENSITY	368 inhabitants per km²
COFFEE PRODUCTION	5,333,000 (60-kilo sacks)
GDP	1,537,966 million US dollars
CURRENCY	Rupee

Sources: *Calendario Atlante De Agostini, 2012*; International Coffee Organization, June 2012

Facing page: the invaluable help of an elephant in a Robusta plantation. Heavy but precise work can only be performed by elephants in forest plantations (southern India, Karnataka, Udeyvar Estate).

Below: the products of a small family estate (natural coffee and chilli peppers).

COFFEE, CHEEK-BY-JOWL WITH FRUIT AND SPICES

It all began during a long, tiring journey around four hundred years ago, when the legendary saint Baba Budan stole seven "magic" coffee beans from Yemen to plant them in the Chandragiri Hills, in Karnataka in southern India.

Then, when the British colonized India, they began exporting the precious crop. The plantations were ravaged by a deadly fungus in 1870, but a fresh Arabica strain was reintroduced in the 1920s and this now accounts for around 50% of the total production (which is almost 5 million 60-kilo sacks). India is the sixth largest producer of coffee in the world, accounting for 4% of the total and, at the same time it is the third largest producer in Asia after Vietnam and Indonesia, where the main crop is Robusta. Indian coffees are obtained through the wet processing method. In other words, the cherries are depulped and left to ferment, before being put out to dry in the sun. Another feature of Indian estates is their reliance on tall trees to protect the coffee plants from the sun's rays.

Below: the register of one of the first Indian plantations, run by the British at the end of the nineteenth century (southern India, Karnataka, Wartyhully Estate).

Facing page: on a coffee plantation, sunlight filters through at sunrise and sunset. For the rest of the day, the plants are protected in the shade of tall trees, with pepper plants twining up their trunks.

The coffee-growing regions of India can be divided into three groups:

- traditional regions, chiefly in southern states: Karnataka, Kerala, Chicmadalur and Tamil Nadu

- non-traditional regions, including Andhra Pradesh and Orissa, in the east of the country

- eastern regions, comprising the so-called "seven sisters": Assam, Manipur, Meghalaya, Mizoram, Tripura, Nagaland and Arunachal Pradesh

Southern plantations are considered the heartland of Indian coffee, centred on the region of Bababudangiris, in Karnataka. Eastern and north-eastern states have witnessed interesting recent experiments with the "black pearl".

Coffee plantations began to multiply in India in the colonial period, in the eighteenth and nineteenth centuries, when land was owned by the British. India is not one of the countries that come first to mind when we think of coffee production, and even though some of the very best Arabica comes from India, the country continues to be associated mainly with tea. However, coffee is extremely popular among the young and more and more are keen to try it.

The Indian government does not earmark subsidies for coffee cultivation in particular and the country exports around two thirds of its crop, mainly to Germany, Italy, Russia and Belgium.

The coffee estates are well designed, with carefully bounded plots, and efficiently run using a minimum of technology. The working day is planned around a logical framework inherited from the British, who applied methodical, rational techniques to establish highly productive plantations, unlike the Spanish – easygoing, but muddleheaded Latins as they were.

The plots belong to small farmers, individual families enjoying high status in Indian society, or industrial giants, such as Tata.

The estates are usually family-run and the holding generally amounts to a few dozen hectares – virtually a field at the back of the house, perhaps next to a vanilla crop – and the work is normally performed by family members themselves. Other members of the community may

A mountain plantation; the land is so steep that pickers have to use ropes to help them reach the plants (southern India, Karnataka, Bidiga Estate).

The processing centre stands out in the middle of this plantation (southern India, Karnataka).

be co-opted in case of need during harvesting. No modern techniques or innovations have been introduced and the rhythms of work follow centuries-old traditions, established when the Indians worked land owned by the British. Coffee growing is a profitable activity and is not very labour intensive, thanks partly to the presence of other crops.

Since coffee plantations are mainly small family businesses (each taking 10 to 100 60-kilo sacks to market each season), there is a sizeable number of coffee exporters, who buy the raw crop directly from the producer before putting it onto the international market; this requires exclusive permits that are hard to obtain. Sampling to check the quality of the coffee and a preliminary wash are normally performed in Hassan.

Over the years, Indians have moved off the land and into the cities in search of the kind of jobs that might not necessarily guarantee a greater income, but are regarded as less menial. Society is still divided rigidly along caste lines and tends to attribute greater status to a city job than to any rural occupation.

Coffee cultivation in India is atypical in that the plants are always grown in conjunction with another crop, such as vanilla, cardamom, pepper and oranges, which means there is something to be harvested throughout the year.

Around fifty different species of tree shade coffee plants in the plantations, helping to prevent erosion on steep slopes

Indian plantations include a variety of crops whose fruit can be gathered throughout the year.

Facing page: gathering cardamom pods.

Right, top: trees planted expressly to provide shade for the coffee shrubs are then used to train pepper, which ripens at a different time of the year; centre: the precious vanilla beans;bottom: ripe coffee beans ready for picking (southern India, Karnataka, Wartyhully Estate).

and enriching the soil with nutrients drawn up from deep below the surface layers. In addition, they serve to protect their charges from seasonal fluctuations in temperature and ensure the area's flora and fauna can thrive.

Indian coffee is considered to be the finest *mild brew* in the world, producing an elegant, enticing beverage with an unmistakeable aroma. Mellow and not too acid, this coffee has an exotic, enveloping

Indian plantations include a huge variety of trees. In the centre of the photo, a tree traditionally thought to be the oldest in the forest, under which the very first coffee plants were bedded out. It is said to be over five hundred years old (southern India, Karnataka, Ossoor Estate).

Double page overleaf: the road linking Hassan to the plantations; the first bus of the morning takes the pickers to their place of work (southern India, Karnataka).

taste and a subtle aroma. The depth of its personality is all due to this policy of protecting the plants beneath a tree canopy.

India has now joined the community of large-scale coffee exporting countries, contributing a range of Arabica varieties, including *Arabica Cherry* and *Monsooned Arabica*, which join *Mysore* and *Malabar* in providing a remarkably full, subtle flavour.

133

Above: before starting the day, the estate foreman organizes the work to be done: clearing the ground, pruning and picking.

Facing page, above: men waiting for the tractor taking them to the various areas of the plantation; below: women on their way to pick coffee cherries (southern India, Karnataka, Ossoor Estate).

Robusta varieties are also grown in India, both because its price makes it good value for money and simply because there is a ready market for it. This variety is grown in areas unsuitable for Arabica, which thrives at altitude, and picking occurs at different times of the year so that they don't interfere with one another and actually makes best use of the machinery and labour force available. The cycle usually begins with Robusta cherries and continues with Arabica, before concluding with the pepper and vanilla harvests.

This *multiple cropping* system enables pickers to turn their attention quickly from coffee to other crops in the plantation, such as pepper, oranges or cardamom – thus virtually ensuring lengthy, though still temporary employment. Besides shading the coffee plants and providing a less aggressive growing regime, multiple cropping also brings a supplementary income, helping plantations to remain economically viable.

Indian cultivations thus imitate the typical layered forest structure, with upper and intermediate layers and a dense undergrowth. In the case of India, all these layers have been created using plants that can generate income and have an agricultural function (providing shade for the coffee plants). Ecological principles have always been followed in Indian farming. The basis of an innovative discipline, which goes by the name of agroecology, has been established simply by following tradition.

PROCESSING METHOD

As in all the countries where coffee grows, the plants flower during the rainy season under the influence of the monsoons, which blow in three-monthly cycles. In the case of India, flowering occurs from May to October and harvesting takes place from October to December and in the months of February and March, during the dry season.

Before picking can begin, an ancient ritual has to be performed each harvest morning in which the names of everyone working in the plantation that day are noted down (always by hand and in ink) in an ornately decorated register. Another feature on coffee estates in India is the use made of elephants, which, flanked by their

Above: the orange crop guard; fruit trees shade the coffee plants, but need to be protected from invasion by monkeys, who are very fond of citrus fruits (southern India, Karnataka, Ossoor Estate).

trainers, gracefully and with great intelligence negotiate the steep hillsides to sort out any heavy work to do with transport or movement. The elephants have a sort of strap in their mouth, which they tie round tree trunks with the aid of their trunks in order to shift the obstruction.

The harvest is entirely hand-picked, which means the cherries are selected one by one. Overripe fruit is also picked because these berries attract pests and can harbour diseases, which could ruin the taste of the coffee in the cup or even kill the plant itself. A berry left to rot on the plant or on the ground beneath it can be home to the notorious *coffee berry borer*, a parasite that gnaws at the fruit and can pave the way to subsequent infection by fungi.

Generally speaking, rather than returning to the plantation with a fresh gang of pickers to collect late-ripening fruit, the whole crop is sometimes picked all in one go, leaving the sorting of ripe and unripe fruit to a later stage.

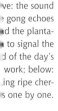

ve: the sound
e gong echoes
d the planta-
 to signal the
d of the day's
work; below:
ing ripe cher-
s one by one.

Above, top: after harvesting, the pickers tie the cherries up in big sacks to be borne off to the processing centres; bottom: a young picker with the fruit of her labours.

Facing page: a guard keeps the crowd of pickers waiting to collect their sacks of coffee beans in order (southern India, Karnataka, Ossoor Estate).

Unripe cherries fetch a lower price but can still be used, although they lend a metallic and astringent flavour to the coffee in the cup.

At around four o'clock in the afternoon, the collecting point echoes to the sound of an ancient gong calling all the pickers scattered throughout the forest to bring in all the cherries they have picked. These have first to be weighed before processing can begin. Each person in the list has the

weight of the cherries picked marked next to his name and will be paid accordingly.

Then rusty old vans take the pickers to where the sorting is to take place. Meanwhile, a battered lorry makes its way along the narrow, muddy lanes in the plantations to load the sacks of coffee beans to be taken to the sorting station. When they arrive, the vehicles are surrounded by a crowd of pickers ready to identify their sacks in an orderly manner. They all line up in a neat queue without making

Double page, overleaf: the sacks are emptied out on the patio of the collecting station, where sorting takes place. Unripe cherries are suitable for the home market and fetch a low price; ripe fruit is washed and sold for export (southern India, Karnataka).

much noise and anxiously wait for the sacks to be handed out. They then empty the sack in a specially marked area in the yard and sit on it to begin the preliminary sorting, which simply separates ripe from unripe cherries. Supervisors keep a watchful eye on proceedings from the walls bounding the yards.

, page, above:
ld scales used
igh the coffee
cted; below: a
elected batch;
eness must be
or the planta-
upervisor may
t the cherries.

cing page: the
-awaited mo-
t of weighing
the individual
atches, sorted
accepted. The
man notes the
t down in the
er against the
ker's name, as
as the agreed
ent (southern
ia, Karnataka,
)ssoor Estate).

The plantations have to be cleared at the end of the harvesting season. Nothing must remain on the plants, so that the rains can trigger a fresh flowering. Harvesting generally takes three months and pickers need to return to the same plant several times to pick only the ripest fruit in order to obtain the best results.

When the sorting is finished, all the sacks are emptied into large containers and taken to be wet processed and depulped. All Indian coffees are washed and in the process conveyed by the water to the pipes that take them to machines that strip the skin and the pulp off the cherries.

Fruit that is not fully ripe is left to dry in the sun and will normally be used to make coffees for the home market. Indians prefer to drink a strong, aromatic drink made from chicory with a little coffee added.

So, all coffees made from unripe cherries are natural (i.e. dried in the sun), while those made from ripe fruit are always washed, fermented and then dried.

The sorting is checked once more during processing. The depulping machines, which strip the skin and part of the pulp off the coffee beans are unable to operate on green cherries, which are too large and too hard. Beans from unripe cherries tend to float in the washing process that takes place after the fermentation stage and separate naturally from top quality beans.

One characteristic of the Indian washing technique is the *soaking* process. After they have fermented, the beans (still wrapped in their parchment) are repeatedly washed in vats of clean water before being dried. It seems that this extra stage makes a considerable difference to the final taste of the coffee as it reduces the coffee's bitterness and astringency. During the process, the beans turn grey, with dark purple undertones.

The coffee beans are then left to dry on concrete patios or on frameworks suspended above the ground, enabling the air to circulate freely. Here graceful, elegantly dressed women wearing bracelets and tinkling anklets stir the beans constantly in order to ensure they dry uniformly. Every evening the

Facing page, below: a fermenting tank for washed beans; above: baskets of still wet beans are emptied onto the drying patio (southern India, Karnataka, Hosurgudda Estate).

Above: the coffee is spread evenly over the patio and left to dry in the sun (southern India, Karnataka, Wartyhully Estate).

147

In order to ensure uniform drying, the coffee has to be turned several times a day (southern India, Karnataka, Hosurgudda Estate).

coffee beans are carefully swept into paral-
lel rows with short brooms before filling the
sacks. Packed away, the coffee can spend
the night safe from the dew. The next morning it will be laid out in the sun once again.
It takes about five or six days for the beans
to dry out completely.

This stage is known as "dry benefit".
This is followed by *polishing*, which removes
the silver skin, making the bean uniform. At
this point it is essential to taste the coffee to
find out if the quality matches the beautiful, shiny appearance.

Facing page: young women gracefully
slide their feet through the beans to
ensure they are properly aired.

Above: the same work can be done
by hand if the coffee is spread onto
raised "beds" to dry; below: the dry
coffee is then swept into piles to make
loading into sacks easier (southern
India, Karnataka, Ossoor Estate).

The coffee can be stirred using wooden rakes to ensure it is dried uniformly (southern India, Karnataka, Hassan, Allana Coffee Curing Works).

153

COFFEE DRINKING, TRADITION VERSUS INNOVATION

The Coffee Cess Committee made the first attempt to promote the sale and consumption of coffee in India in November 1935. Following this, the first India Coffee House opened in Bombay on 28 September 1936.

The coffee industry was liberalized in 1996 and this made a significant difference to how farmers, exporters and retailers went about their business. The coffee retail trade in India is now booming as never before. Some traditional roasters have revamped their retail outlets, while newcomers have experimented with novelties and offer a vast range of ground or unground roasted coffees.

The spread of the taste for coffee in India has been taken as one of the most visible signs of a booming economy.

Facing page, below: a dark, dry warehouse containing jute sacks coffee (southern India, Karnataka, ...tyhully Estate); ...ight, and facing page, above: ...ndreds of highly ...rienced women ...check the beans ...e by one before ...ey are exported (southern India, ...nataka, Hassan, Allana Coffee Curing Works).

The India Coffee House chain was extreme-ly popular between the 1940s and 1970s, reaching a peak of 72 premises, which be-came the natural meeting place for a whole generation.

Café Coffee Day (CCD), the leading *coffee shop* group at the moment, has a huge network of over 400 shops throughout the country and after moving into retailing in 1996, the company opened two cafés in Austria, in Vienna, and another in Karachi, in Pakistan.

Indians tend to prefer cappuccino or filter coffee to espresso and the blends of-fered are naturally adapted to suit this taste. Teaching Indians how to make a good coffee at home is another promising avenue since a sketchy understanding of the correct proce-dure puts people off drinking coffee in their own homes.

Facing page, above: the lighting in the sorting hall is carefully designed to provide the perfect condition for checking the beans; below: discarded beans are tossed into the basket to be sold on the home market.

Right: plants are watered by hand. Constant care and attention ensure a top quality product and there is no shortage of willing workers in India (southern India, Karnataka, Hassan, Allana Coffee Curing Works).

FULL NAME	República Federativa do Brasil (Federal Republic of Brazil)
CAPITAL	Brasilia (2,570,160 inhabitants)
OFFICIAL LANGUAGE	Portuguese
GOVERNMENT	federal republic
INDEPENDENCE	1822
SURFACE	8,502,728 km^2
POPULATION	190,755,799 (2010 census)
DENSITY	22 inhabitants per km^2
COFFEE PRODUCTION	43,484,000 (60-kilo sacks)
GDP	2,090,314 million US dollars
CURRENCY	Brazilian Real

Sources: *Calendario Atlante De Agostini*, 2012; International Coffee Organization, June 2012

Facing page: a Brazilian farmer in the Minas Gerais region (Monte Carmelo).

Below: a typical Brazilian estate in the Minas Gerais region (São Gotardo).

FROM TOKEN OF LOVE TO PRECIOUS FRUIT

Brazil is the fifth largest country in the world. It covers almost half of South America and shares a border with all the countries on the continent, except Chile and Ecuador.

Flying over the country, it is easy to see what coffee means to Brazil. This little, cherry-like fruit, bright red when ripe, is essential to the country's economy and is deeply respected and cared for by the locals.

Coffee was introduced into Brazil thanks to the efforts of Portuguese sergeant major Francisco de Mello Palheta. The story goes that in 1727 the governor general of Maranhão and Gran Parà, João de Maria Gama, decided to send his trusted soldier to help the French governor D'Orvilliers and arbitrate in a border dispute between French and Dutch Guyana. Palheta settled the matter to everyone's satisfaction and was promptly invited by D'Orvilliers to visit his famous coffee plantations.

The soldier became great friends with the governor's wife, Mme Claude,

Clockwise, above: the old auction room in the coffee exchange in Santos (Brazil), now a museum; the entrance to the coffee exchange; a monument commemorating coffee haulers at the port of Santos (Brazil), from where almost all Brazil's export coffee is shipped; the drying area in a *fazenda* in the Minas Gerais region (Pocos de Caldas).

and when he left she gave him a handful of seeds of the precious plant (apparently slipped into his pocket by the lady herself) and a large bunch of flowers, among which were hidden some coffee seedlings. Once home in Belém do Pará, Palheta planted the seedlings and started the process that would lead to Brazil becoming the world's largest producer of coffee.

Commanding officer João Alberto Castelo Branco was responsible for extending coffee cultivation further afield. It was his merchant ship that took plants from Maranhão to the south of the country around Rio de Janeiro, leaving them in the hands of the Capuchin Fathers, turning Rio into the first coffee capital. Brazil was a Portuguese colony and it is said that even King John VI (who ruled from 1816 to 1826) distributed coffee seeds to members of his court to encourage them to set up their own estates. In the state of São João Marcos, the Marquis of Lavradio even exempted those growing coffee from military service.

Coffee cultivation developed rapidly in Brazil from 1810 and by 1826 coffee exports had grown from virtually nil at the beginning of the century to 20% of total world production. Indeed it was in this century that coffee outstripped cane sugar as the country's main export product.

Having arrived on the continent in search of gold, the Portuguese had to turn themselves into merchants, trading in maize, milk and other foodstuffs, becoming so rich in the process that they were able to invest much of their profits in coffee plantations. The abolition of slavery in 1888 was the signal for thousands of European emigrants (mainly Italians) to head for Brazil to work in the *fazendas* (plantations). By 1889 Brazil was able to boast of being the world's leading coffee producer, forcing Java into second place. With Brazil becoming the chief market of the Portuguese, the *fazendeiros* began to

wield enormous power. In order to keep them sweet, the authorities started to confer on these large landowners the title of baron.

The state of Rio, home to the capital and the largest coffee producer in the country, was overtaken by São Paulo in 1886. Then in 1928 it also fell behind Minas Gerais, and in 1928, behind the state of Espírito Santo, and is at present in fourth place among the country's producers. Coffee is now grown in the states of São Paulo, Paraná, Minas Gerais, Espírito Santo, Rio de Janeiro, Bahia, Goiás, Pernambuco, Mato Grosso, Mato Grosso do Sul, Ceará and Rondônia. The Great Depression of 1929 affected the entire world economy and one of its effects in Brazil was to weaken the hold the estate owners had on the government, leading to the formation of an opposition movement known as the "Liberal Alliance", which had the support of nationalist officers.

By 1960, coffee alone accounted for 50-55% of the country's GDP, a figure which has since been pegged back to 3-4%. This means that only a small proportion of

Above: Joaqu[...]
C. Dias's faze[...]
village, with [...]
amenities, ap[...]
out of nowhe[...]
the picking se[...]

Left: rows of [...]
trees, which a[...]
allowed to gr[...]
to around thr[...]
metres in Bra[...]

Facing page: [...]
stripping, i.e. [...]
manually rem[...]
all the beans [...]
a branch irre[...]
of ripeness (E[...]
Minas Gerais [...]
Poços de Cal[...]

Brazil's economy is based on the coffee industry, but should the country decide to cease production, the impact across the world would be considerable since Brazilian coffee represents the 33% of world production (source: International Coffee Organization, June 2012).

COFFEE: BRAZILIAN GOLD

Over 43 million. This is the number of 60-kilo sacks that Brazil produced in 2011 out of a world total of about 131 million (source: International Coffee Organization, June 2012). Coffee thus has an extremely important place in the country's economy.

The estates are so neatly planted and huge as to take the breath away; the coffee plants grow in rows like ranks

of little soldiers, often lined up in the shade of giant trees. *Coffea* has found an ideal habitat in this country and the fruit it produces is of the highest quality.

Arabica is the species cultivated and the plants grow vigorously to two to three metres in height and are sometimes helped to overcome the hottest periods of the year by highly advanced systems of irrigation or a wide range of shade-producing shrubs and trees.

Producers take advantage of the most advanced technology through the entire life cycle of the plant and in the processing of the fruit. In the picking season landowners (whether large, medium or small) can seek the help of one of the many cooperatives offering advice on agricultural matters and providing special funding. These cooperatives were set up after 1932 to stabilize prices and provide a quality control mechanism and often buy coffee directly from the farmers, who retain their independence. Green coffee beans are sometimes bought by the cooperatives as *bica corrida*, coffee which has not undergone any type of selection process.

Facing page,
above: the cherries
are sifted after
picking to remove
leaves, twigs and
pebbles; below,
freshly picked
Arabica coffee.

Right: metal
buckets are the unit
of measurement
used to calculate
the crop in this
estate instead
of weighing the
cherries (Brazil,
Minas Gerais
region, Pocos
de Caldas).

Above: owing to differences in specific
weight, running water can be used to
separate ripe, unripe and fermented
cherries naturally.

Facing page: one of the many ways
to spread the coffee (in this case the
Bourbon variety of natural Arabica)
over the patio of the *fazenda*, where
it is left to dry in the sun.

Below: the cherries need to be constantly
aired on the patio (Brazil, Minas Gerais
region, Pocos de Caldas).

Coffee drying in a large
lowland plantation (Brazil,
Minas Gerais region,
Monte Carmelo).

Today, 2-3% of producers (mainly those who work large plantations) sell privately; around 80% are small farms that prefer to sell through the cooperatives. During the picking season, consortiums can handle up to one thousand samples of coffee a day.

Growing coffee in Brazil means being a landowner, however small the holding might be. It's a profitable business and it is quickly returning to the prominence it enjoyed in the past. The slump in the 1990s led to greater stress being laid on quality rather than quantity. Growers have begun to accept a lower yield in return for a better product. Even the older farmers, who tend to be stuck in traditional ways, have come to appreciate that the way forward is to find new ways to improve the standard of the beans taken to market. This means that Brazilians do not turn their backs on innovative fertilizers and modern machinery and are ready to seek advice from agronomists to produce a better crop.

Facing page: mechanical irrigation in a plantation. These arms can be up to 500 metres long.

Above: the estates are sometimes so huge that the only way to pick the crop is by mechanized means (Brazil, Minas Gerais region, São Gotardo).

They drum the importance of education into the heads of their children and grandchildren and encourage them to study anything to do with the business, from agricultural science to engineering, economics and business management, so as to be as competitive as possible.

Tough and proud, like their coffee plants, Brazilian landowners are known for their patience and resilience, as well as for their willingness to embrace the new with energy and conviction in the effort to improve their plantations.

Above: before it is sold, the coffee is electronically sorted by a colour-sensitive machine able to detect faulty beans.

Below: a huge coffee-drying patio.

Facing page, above: drying the coffee (Brazil, Minas Gerais region, Monte Carmelo).

Colombia

FULL NAME	República de Colombia (Republic of Colombia)
CAPITAL	Bogotá (8,493,675 inhabitants)
OFFICIAL LANGUAGE	Spanish
GOVERNMENT	presidential republic
INDEPENDENCE	1810 (declared), 1822 (recognized by Spain)
SURFACE	1,141,748 km²
POPULATION	45,508,205 (2010 estimate)
DENSITY	40 inhabitants per km²
COFFEE PRODUCTION	7,800,000 (60-kilo sacks)
GDP	285,511 million US dollars (2010)
CURRENCY	Colombian Peso

Sources: *Calendario Atlante De Agostini*, 2012; International Coffee Organization, June 2012

Facing page: the result of careful hand *picking*, in which the cherries are picked one by one (Colombia, department of Cauca, Popayan municipality).

Below: a view of the Rio Negro valley, with typical Colombian mountain vegetation.

Colombia takes its name from Christopher Columbus and the locals turn it into the amusing spoonerism *Locombia*, crazy land. This craziness also translates into a series of wonderful landscapes where a mass of colours all come together to extraordinary effect, from the white of the superb beaches and the mesmeric blue of the Caribbean Sea to the luscious green of the Amazonian jungle and the glittering white of the snowy peaks of the Andes.

Colombia has one of the most varied floras and faunas in South America and this is echoed in the variety of ethnic groups that live there, representing as they do many of the characteristics present in the other countries in Latin America. This land is perhaps little known and tends to be associated immediately with drug smugglers and guerrilla fighters, as well as the two most famous emeralds in the world, both unearthed in Colombian mines: the *Devonshire*, weighing over one thousand carats, and the *Patricia*, described by experts as "an emerald too perfect to be cut". But it's a land that deserves to be savoured for all its many facets; one of the most exotic, sensual, wild and enchanting countries one could visit.

CAFÉ DE COLOMBIA: THE SWEETEST OF PGI COFFEES

Colombia is the fourth largest producer of coffee in the world, accounting for 6% of the total and it is the second producer of Arabica after Brazil. Coffee cultivation depends on a number of factors, such as the environment (including soil and climate), the use of fertilizers, the economic resources available, the potential yield of the individual plants, their resistance to disease and lastly how well men look after them.

Colombian coffee is grown at high altitude and the plants are shaded by the broad leaves of banana and rubber trees. The main Arabica varieties grown in Colombia are highly sought after and include *Caturra, Typica, Bourbon, Maragogype, Tabi* and *Castillo*, producing a smooth, moderately bitter coffee with pronounced acidity and aroma. Among these it is important to distinguish the tall-growing from the low shrub varieties.

Examples of tall-growing varieties include *Typica*, whose beans are bronze or reddish and *Bourbon*, which tends towards green. *Tabi* (which means "good" in the Colombian dialect) is a cross between *Typica, Bourbon* and the hybrid *Timor*, which makes Arabica more resistant and lends a greater aroma to Robusta.

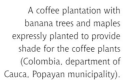

A coffee plantation with banana trees and maples expressly planted to provide shade for the coffee plants (Colombia, department of Cauca, Popayan municipality).

Above: the headquarters of the Federación Nacional de Cafeteros, in Cartagena. The federation was established in 1927 to provide advice to Colombian coffee farmers and to coordinate and protect their work.

The chief shrub varieties are *Caturra* and *Castillo*: both provide high yields and produce an excellent cup of coffee.

It takes a skilfully judged blend of these varieties to deserve the *Café de Colombia* PGI (Protected Geographical Indication) label, indicating a coffee characterized by its subtlety, medium-high acidity, good body and full, emphatic roast almond aroma.

The cultivation, processing, transport and trading of coffee provides a living for a large proportion of the population: there are more than 570,000 *cafeteros* (coffee growers, representing 22% of the total Colombian labour force), mostly members of the Federación Nacionalde Cafeteros (FNC), the Colombian Coffee Federation. This organization has been helping Colombian farmers for over eighty years, keeping market prices steady and ensuring the high quality of the coffee sold.

One thing that makes Colombian coffee unique is the special link between farmers and the national federation. This body was established in 1927 by a group of farmers wishing to set up a mutual aid society and the result is a non-profit, apolitical cooperative providing farmers with social assistance and supporting them in their agricultural projects. The aim is to stabilize and consolidate the Colombian coffee market and to ensure a high standard of coffee.

Thanks to government supervision and carefully judged export taxes, the federation manages to shelter farmers from sudden collapses in the price of coffee.

When the price falls below a pre-established minimum, the federation freezes all trading, buys up the crop and stores it, releasing it onto the market only when the price has risen to a sustainable level.

The federation is not concerned only with coffee, but also helps fund social programmes and builds schools, roads and aqueducts to improve the standard of living of the over four million Colombians whose livelihood depends on coffee.

In Colombia, the federation now incorporates over 500,000 small and independent *cafeteros*, who own smallholdings of two hectares on average. The farmers are thus protected from excessive price fluctuations which can occur on the international market and their strength lies in being able to act almost like a single large company, in the protective embrace of the federation.

Other important crops in the country include cane sugar, rice, bananas, tobacco and cotton, while cereals, vegetables and a wide range of tropical fruits and flowers are of lesser importance. Animal

Above: an agronomist from the Federación Nacional de Cafeteros wearing its uniform. These figures are highly respected and a local adage says it all: "Don't shoot at the yellow shirts!" (Colombia, department of Cauca, Popayan municipality).

Right: a forest plantation; the soil is always damp, so there is no need for irrigation.

Facing page, above: hand *picking* only the best red cherries.

Below: animals unwittingly help the farmers by eating the grass and providing perfect natural fertilizer (Colombia, department of Santander, San Gil).

husbandry, involving large numbers of cattle, pigs, sheep and horses, some for export, is another significant component in Colombia's agriculture.

In Colombia, coffee is picked almost the year round, although the main picking season stretches from October to December, with another between April and June. Colombian coffee is sought after for its acid notes and is grown at altitudes ranging from 1000 to 2000 metres, where the average temperature is 20 degrees centigrade and rainfall is plentiful, reaching 2300 millilitres per year.

There are two main coffee growing areas: one in central Colombia, around Medellin, Armenia and Manizales (also known as MAM), which produces a

Above: leaving a plot to lie fallow creates the best conditions for the next coffee crop.

Facing page: a view from the famous Panamerican Highway, the road linking Mexico to Tierra del Fuego, in Argentina. A long stretch hugs the Rio Negro valley in Colombia.

full-bodied coffee with a strong aroma carefully balanced between acid and bitter; the eastern part of the country, around Bogotá and Bucaramanga, is more mountainous and produces a more subtle, less acid coffee. This region grows the finest coffees.

The region known as Viejo Caldas (Old Caldas) extends over the Andes, the Sierra Nevada de Santa Marta and the Serraina de la Macarena, to the south of the department of Antioquia, and is now divided into three departments: Caldas, Risaralda and Quindio. This is a key coffee-growing area and developed over the past century when, exasperated by the endless series of civil wars that had ravaged the region, entire families from Antioquia packed their bags and headed off to virgin territories to found new cities.

Above: the hilly roads in a village inhabited mainly by farmers (Colombia, department of Santander, San Gil).

Right: cleaning a patio in a processing centre (Colombia, department of Santander, San Gil).

Coffee has adapted perfectly to the region's ideal mountainous and climatic conditions. The soil is a mixture of humus and particles of ancient volcanic rocks, combining fertility with excellent drainage. Coffees from this region account for the majority of the country's annual production.

The landscape where the coffee is grown is often astonishingly beautiful. Nestling between the coffee and banana plantations are the distinctive buildings of the local farms, surrounded by huge gar-

A proud Colombian plantation owner (Colombia, department of Santander, San Gil).

dens full of flowers. The "colonial architecture" of the more humble houses in the small towns is also full of charm and lends a special flavour to this whole area.

Latin America in general is a multicoloured, cheerful world, which is perhaps chaotic but also full of life. When you arrive in Colombia, you realise why this is so: bright, primary colours are set side by side and the effect is powerful enough to turn your eyes skywards, where the clouds seem to be in relief against the impossibly blue sky. Everything around appears to have clearly defined colours and outlines, making the dark mountains topped with grey clouds that surround the area recede into the background.

In a patchwork landscape it is not easy to tell where one house ends and another begins; the roads resignedly follow the inevitably undulating contours of a land where nothing is flat and the mischievous climate cuts from shower to sunshine with no warning.

FROM PLANT
TO BEAN

In Colombia, coffee beans are wet processed, producing a washed coffee. There are three main stages in the whole procedure: picking, *benefit* and stripping of the parchment, the whitish membrane enveloping the coffee bean (the process is called *hulling*).

Colombian coffee plants start life in a *nursery*, where thousands of carefully selected beans are stored away from the harmful effects of sudden changes in temperature until they are ready to be planted in rich, fertile soil. About eight weeks after sowing the seedlings sprout in full sunlight and the most vigorous are placed in shaded areas, where they remain for around six months. At this point they will be two metres tall and can be bedded out in the plantation proper.

It takes three to four years for a

Facing page: these cherries are ready for picking.

Above: a spontaneous shoot sprouting from a coffee seed (Colombia, department of Cauca, Popayan municipality).

plant to produce the first cherries. Flowering is triggered by heavy rainfall and since this is a tropical region, it rains frequently and consequently flowers are constantly blooming. So any given shrub can have cherries of varying colours, indicating the different degrees of ripeness. Picking is a crucial stage, because it is essential to pick only the ripest cherries to ensure a coffee of excellent quality. The fruit is usually picked 7-8 months after flowering.

Facing page: picker at work.

Above: a coffee sapling.

Below: a branch with ripe cherries.

The next step is the *benefit*, which involves stripping the pulp, cleaning, fermentation, washing and drying.

The depulper, which removes the pulp surrounding the coffee bean, is the only machinery used by Colombian farmers.

The pulp and skin are later used as fertilizer, while the beans, still enveloped in their parchment, are conveyed towards large concrete *tanks* full of cool water and soaked for twenty-four hours, when they are allowed to ferment for a short time. The beans are then washed with the aid of large rakes which eliminate every last twig or piece of foreign matter, and after washing they are ready to be dried in the sun. They are loaded into big straw baskets and taken to be spread out over concrete patios.

Facing page:
branch heavily
loaded with
ripe Arabica
cherries of the
characteristically
bright yellow
bourbon variety;
the plants
sometimes grow
in the shade of
giant bamboo.

Right: pickers
returning from
a day's work
(Colombia,
department of
Cauca, Popayan
municipality).

The coffee beans are arranged in layers no more than 2-3 centimetres deep and have to be turned over frequently in order to ensure a uniform degree of humidity and to avoid unwanted fermentation. As a further precaution, they are covered with a tarpaulin at night or in case of rain.

After depulping and drying, the coffee beans are put into coarse canvas sacks and loaded onto jeeps. In some areas, mules and donkeys are still the preferred method of transporting the crop to market, where a sample of beans from the batch is tested for quality.

Only at the end of this long process will the federation put its seal of approval on the sack. However, before the sacks are sealed for good, another sample is taken,

Facing page: coffee drying in the sun in a small family estate.

Above: frequent showers make it hard to dry the coffee properly, so sliding corrugated iron roofs are used to protect the beans, ensuring they are aired.

Below: a jute sack with the coffee's origin clearly stamped on it (Colombia, department of Cauca, Popayan municipality).

Above, from left: samples of the various high quality Colombian coffees; an expert examines the defects in a coffee sample, before the beans are sent to possible buyers (Colombia, port of Cartagena).

Below: jute sacks in a warehouse in the port of Cartagena.

roasted, ground and used to prepare a coffee so that its aroma and taste can be assessed. Should the expert not be satisfied with the quality of a given batch, they have the power to stop it being exported.

The last stage consists in marking the variety of coffee and its provenance on each sack, thus certifying its origin.

The busy quays in the port of Cartagena (Colombia).

Coffee in the kitchen

THE RECIPES
OF GIANFRANCO VISSANI

It's all a question of habits, time-honoured rituals and customs that are part of everyday life: coffee is a beverage. It may be an espresso served in a café, a carefully prepared cup of moka or a *mug* of American filter coffee, but it is certainly never considered an ingredient, unless it is to be used in cakes, ice-cream, mousses or Bavarian creams.

Gianfranco Vissani has his own take on coffee beans, giving them prominence in sweets and savouries and experimenting with astonishing combinations that captivate at the very first taste.

The flavour, fragrance and texture of the food blend with the aroma of coffee in a perfect equilibrium, creating a harmony that titillates the palate and at the same time makes the taste buds sit up by the unaffected and unexpected originality of these creations. Meat, fish, vegetables, chocolate: you have only to choose where to begin on your journey into a gastronomic and culinary experience that is unique and... repeatable.

GRILLED TOMINO CHEESE WITH CHAMPIGNON SALAD, CREAMED BLACK COD WITH ORANGE AND COFFEE-FLAVOURED BUTTER

INGREDIENTS FOR FOUR

- 4 tomino cheeses
- 100 grams champignon mushrooms
- 150 grams black cod
- 100 grams potatoes
- grated orange peel
- extra virgin olive oil to taste
- 3 garlic cloves
- 2 bay leaves
- black peppercorns to taste
- 100 grams butter
- one espresso coffee
- vegetable bouillon to taste

PREPARATION

Boil the potatoes in their skins and boil the cod for ten minutes in a separate saucepan, adding a clove of garlic, the bay leaves and black peppercorns. Meanwhile, blend the butter with the espresso coffee.

Peel the potatoes and put them in a blender with the boiled cod and oil (flavoured with two fried cloves of garlic) and blend until you have an even-textured, light mixture. Add salt and pepper to taste together with the grated orange peel.

Grill the tomino cheeses. In the meantime, slice the champignons finely and melt the coffee-flavoured butter gently in a small pan, whisking it with a little bouillon.

Pour the butter on a dish and lay the grilled tomino, cod and sliced mushrooms on it.

CALAMINT-SCENTED ARTICHOKE TART, WITH ANCHOVY, COFFEE AND LEMON SAUCE

INGREDIENTS FOR FOUR

For the tart
- 4 artichokes
- 200 grams à *foncer** pastry
- one egg
- 100 grams cream
- 2 garlic cloves
- 2 sticks of calamint
- one bay leaf
- 1 spoonful grated grana cheese

For the sauce
- 25 cl vegetable bouillon
- 1 gram coffee powder
- 5 cl lemon juice
- 2 salted anchovy fillets
- 15 grams shallots
- one bay leaf
- oil, salt and pepper to taste

PREPARATION

For the tart: wash the artichokes and cut them into thin segments; fry lightly in oil with the garlic, bay leaf and calamint, ensuring the artichokes remain slightly crisp.
Put the pastry mix in a mould and add the artichokes, covering them with a mixture made up of the cream, egg, grana cheese, salt and pepper. Bake for 15 minutes at 160°C.

For the sauce: fry the finely chopped shallots in oil with the garlic, bay leaf, anchovies, coffee and lemon; pour in the bouillon and cook for a few minutes.
Take out the bay leaf and garlic and remove the pan from the source of heat; blend in a mixer and strain through a *chinoise* (a cone-shaped strainer, consisting of a metal-meshed cone wholly or partly made of steel, used for straining or filtering food).
Thin or thicken as necessary and salt to taste.

* à *foncer* pastry is made from 250 grams flour, 200 grams butter, one egg and salt to taste. Sift the flour into a pyramid and put the egg, a pinch of salt and the butter in the middle. Knead until you have a compact, even dough. Put in the fridge for at least an hour.

LAMB WITH MIREPOIX OF SCALLOPS, BLACK TRUFFLES AND FOIE-GRAS, WITH MANGO AND LAMB GRAVY SAUCE AND FIELD CHICORY AND COFFEE FLAN

INGREDIENTS FOR FOUR

For the lamb
- rack of lamb
- garlic and rosemary and lard to rub on the lamb

For the mirepoix
- 25 grams scallops
- 20 grams black truffles
- 25 grams *foie-gras*

For the sauce
- 30 grams mango
- 50 grams lamb gravy*
- 2 garlic cloves
- 2 bay leaves
- 15 grams chopped shallots
- 25 cl vegetable bouillon
- extra virgin olive oil, salt and pepper to taste

For the flan
- 160 grams coffee-flavoured chicory puree**
- one egg and one yolk
- 20 grams cream
- 15 grams flour
- 20 grams butter

PREPARATION

For the lamb: rub the garlic, rosemary and lard over the lamb. Add salt, pepper and oil. Put in the oven at 160° for at least one hour.

For the mirepoix: cut the scallops, truffles and *foie-gras* into cubes as evenly sized as possible and heat them quickly in a non-stick pan and put them on a plate in layers.

For the sauce: fry the chopped shallots with the garlic and bay leaf. Add the finely chopped mango and lamb gravy and cook for a few minutes. Add the vegetable bouillon and as soon as it boils, remove the garlic and bay leaf, put in a mixer and then strain through a *chinoise* (a cone-shaped strainer, consisting of a metal-meshed cone wholly or partly made of steel, used for straining or filtering food).

For the flan: blend the egg yolks with the chicory puree and add the flour, butter, cream and lastly the whipped egg white. Bake at 250°C for three minutes.

* For the lamb gravy: brown the bones in the oven, then put them in a saucepan with carrots, onions and celery. If desired, add herbs and a splash of white wine. Cover with water and cook for a long time allowing the liquid to foam. When it has been reduced by half, discard the bones and put into a mixer. Return to the saucepan and continue to reduce on a very low flame.

** Cook the chicory in very little water, adding a double espresso or a moka coffee for three. Strain and puree in a mixer.

MANGO FLAN WITH VANILLA-FLAVOURED ZOLFINO BEAN PUREE AND COFFEE AND WHITE CHOCOLATE SAUCE

INGREDIENTS FOR FOUR

For the flan
- 2 yolks
- 4 egg whites
- 120 grams sugar
- 30 grams flour
- 120 grams mango puree
- 80 grams melted butter
- 50 grams white chocolate

For the zolfino bean puree
- 100 grams zolfino beans
- 20 grams icing sugar
- one stick of vanilla

For the sauce
- 180 grams white chocolate
- 100 grams espresso or moka coffee
- 250 grams cream
- 30 cl coffee liqueur

PREPARATION

For the flan: whip the sugar with the yolks, add the melted white chocolate, melted butter, mango puree, flour and lastly the whipped egg whites. Bake at around 240°C for 5 or 6 minutes.

For the puree: boil the zolfino beans and strain, add the sugar and the stick of vanilla broken in two; mix vigorously for a few minutes on a very low flame.

For the sauce: melt the white chocolate in a bain-marie, adding the coffee, cream and liqueur; mix thoroughly with a whisk and keep warm.

Pour the coffee and white chocolate sauce in the centre of a plate; make a *quenelle* with the zolfino puree by passing it from one spoon to another so it becomes oblong; put the boiling flan in the centre. Decorate the dish with flakes of white chocolate.

Glossary

american roast – american roast – coffee roasted for the American market, medium brown colour.

American, coffee – a filter coffee.

Arabian mocha – a coffee variety from the southwest of the Arabian peninsula, grown in the mountains of Yemen along the Red Sea. This is believed to be the oldest cultivated coffee and is distinguished by a full, enveloping body and wine-like, acidic undertones.

Arabica (Coffea arabica) – the first species to be cultivated and the most widely grown throughout the world. It represents around 60% of world production and has a complex, balanced aroma.

Blend – a variable number of varieties of coffee bean ground together, the species may be the same or different (Arabica and Robusta).

Bourbon – botanical variety of Arabica appearing on the island of Bourbon (now Réunion). Many of the finest Latin American coffees are Bourbons.

Caffeine – an odourless, bitter alkaloid (organic substance) responsible for the stimulating properties of tea and coffee.

Cherry – the fruit of the coffee plant. It looks very like the familiar cherry, being bright red when ripe. The two beans lying one in front of the other within are enveloped in a sugary pulp and a tough skin.

Decaffeination – this process eliminates much of the caffeine in green coffee beans. In Italy a decaffeinated coffee cannot contain over 0.1% caffeine, by law. There are various systems, using water, an organic solvent or carbon dioxide in a hypercritical state.

Defects – unpleasant smells or tastes caused by errors in picking, drying, storing or transport of the coffee beans. The most common include: too many unripe or overripe cherries, fermentation of the pulp and infection by micro-organisms, other interrupted processes (sun-drying or wet processing), storage in a damp or excessively hot place, faulty roasting.

Espresso – may refer to either the type of roast, or the type of coffee in the cup (25-30 millilitres), in which water at 88-92°C is forced at 9 atmospheres through a filter containing the ground coffee.

Fazenda – plantation.

Fermentation (process) – in wet processing, natural enzymes attack the skin and pulp of the cherry, stripping them from the beans wrapped in a sugary mucilage.

Filter coffee – a mild type of coffee: the ground coffee is poured into a funnel-shaped paper filter and hot water is poured over it.

Flavoured (coffees) – roasted coffee blends with added flavourings (vanilla, chocolate, caramel, etc.).

Green coffee – raw, unroasted coffee beans.

Overextracted, espresso – a dark crema, with a white patch in the centre, is typical of an overextracted coffee, which contains more caffeine and has a bitter, astringent taste. The causes may be high temperature and/or pressure, or prolonged extraction, sometimes due to an excessive quantity of coffee or fine grind, leading the cup to be filled too slowly.

Parchment – a tough, thick membrane covering coffee beans within the cherry.

Peaberry – a small, round cherry which may appear at the end of high branches on the coffee plant, containing only one bean instead of the usual two.

Percolation – method of producing coffee in the cup by passing water through a cake of ground coffee.

Percolator – a machine producing a very mild coffee in the cup: water passes through the ground coffee exclusively through the force of gravity.

Processing, dry – removal of the skins and pulp enclosing the beans through drying. When only ripe fruit is used and the drying is performed correctly, the coffee is complex, fruity and well-structured. But when the picking and drying are not carried out properly, as in the cheaper coffees, the coffee tastes sour and astringent.

Processing, wet – removal of the skin and pulp enclosing the beans while still wet. Nearly all the finest coffees in the world are wet processed, which generally increases acidity, in this case a positive attribute. The process involves stripping the skin mechanically and transferring the remains to tanks where natural enzymes attack the pulp. The beans are then washed in abundant running water.

Processing, wet and dry – this procedure shares certain features of both methods, as the skin and pulp are removed mechanically and the beans are dried, but retain a little mucilage and the parchment.

Robusta (*Coffea canephora*) – the name is derived from the plant's natural resilience: it grows at low altitudes and is high-yielding. The liquor is full-bodied and slightly tart compared to Arabica and contains a higher proportion of caffeine.

Sack – jute sacks containing green coffee; the standard weight is around 60 kilos, but this can vary from country to country.

Turkish coffee – very finely ground coffee boiled in water, sugar is added and the coffee is poured into cups without filtering.

Underextracted, espresso – a light-coloured crema is a sign of an underextracted espresso, which is acidic and lacking body. This can be due to low temperature and/or pressure, or short preparation, sometimes due to insufficient coffee or coarse grind, leading the cup to be filled too quickly.

Weak – coffee with insufficient body in the cup.

AROMAS AND SCENTS

Acrid – this is a negative note found mainly in coffees with the so-called "rio" defect. These coffees have a sour, pungent taste due to an excess of salts and acids, leading to an acid imbalance.

Animal – an odour reminiscent of animals. It is not a fragrant aroma like musk but has the characteristic odour of wet fur, sweat, leather or urine.

Burnt/smoky – similar to the smell found in burnt food. The odour is associated with smoke produced when burning wood. This negative, bitter note is typical of over-roasted or overextracted coffees.

Caramel – a smell of heated sugar, like fudge. It is due to the changes sugars undergo during roasting. It is important not to use this descriptor when speaking of burnt notes.

Cereal, malty, toast-like – This descriptor includes aromas characteristic of cereal, malt, and toast. It includes scents such as the aroma and flavour of unbaked bread or roasted grain.

Chemical, medicinal – This odour descriptor is reminiscent of chemicals, medicines and the smell of hospitals. This term is used to describe coffees having aromas such as rio flavour.

Chocolate-like – reminiscent of the aroma and fragrance of cocoa powder and dark and milk chocolate. It is close to unsweetened vanilla-flavoured cocoa and is typical of some varieties of Arabica, especially those from Central America.

Earthy – The characteristic odour of damp or wet soil. Sometimes associated with a raw potato flavour.

Fermented – a negative descriptor, noticeable when the sugars in a cherry have begun to ferment. The coffee tastes of mould, earth and rotten fruit.

Floral – smells of flowers (especially jasmine).

Fruity – recalling the smell and taste typical of red fruit. One must take care not to use this descriptor when describing the aroma of unripe or overripe coffees.

Grassy – redolent of freshly mown grass, leaves or seeds and unripe fruit.

Hazelnut – the smell of fresh hazelnuts (not to be confused with rancid walnuts) and not the bitter taste of almonds.

Leather – a negative note caused by excessive heat in the drying process after picking or faulty storage.

Rancid – recalling the smell of rancid butter and the oxidation of several other products.

Rio – due to the presence of micro-organisms during the drying process. It is a medicinal smell associated with the same substance (trichloroanisole) that causes wine to smell of cork.

Rubber – the odour of overheated tyres and rubber objects. A strong characteristic note.

Smoky – the smell of an ashtray, the fingers of a smoker, the scene of a fire. Tasters use this term to describe the degree of roasting.

Spicy – this descriptor is typical of the odour of sweet spices such as cloves and cinnamon, but does not apply to the sharp, pungent smells of a curry.

Tobacco – fresh rather than burning tobacco.

Winey – found when there is a strong note of acidity or fruit. Used to describe the combined sensation of smell, taste and mouthfeel experienced when drinking wine.

Woody – reminiscent of the smell of wet wood, an oak barrel, or cardboard.

TASTE

Acidity – a positive note when referring to taste and found in Arabica coffees, it is due to organic acids combining with sugars; if it is more intense and is not linked to taste, it can refer to the pH and the changes in some of the components in coffee leading to negative, unwanted sour notes.

Bitterness – a taste derived especially from over-roasted coffees or high temperatures during extraction; a hint of bitterness can be a positive attribute.

Sweetness – this note is lent to the coffee by the caramelised sugars forming during correct roasting; prolonging the roasting leads to the note diminishing and disappearing altogether. Commonly associated with sweet aroma descriptors such as fruity, chocolate and caramel.

MOUTHFEEL

Astringency – typical of unripe persimmon or raw artichoke; this sensation is produced by tannins, substances of vegetable origin that cause the mucin content in saliva to drop suddenly, resulting in a dry mouth. This is typical of poor-quality coffees and overextracted espresso.

Body – used to describe the physical properties of the beverage and is associated with sensations of fullness, roundness, richness and denseness.

Photografic Credits

Maurizio Cargnelli
pages: 26, 29 top, 29 bottom, 31, 34, 35 left, 35 right, 36, 39 right, 44, 57, 66, 74, 90, 102, 103 bottom, 125, 127, 129, 131 top, 131 centre, 131 bottom, 134-135, 137 top, 139 bottom, 140 top, 140 bottom, 142-143, 144 bottom, 146 bottom, 150, 151 top, 152-153, 156 bottom, 157, 158, 159, 161 top, 161 centre, 161 bottom, 162-163 top, 162 bottom, 164 top, 164 bottom, 166-167, 167 top, 170, 171, 181 top, 183, 184 top, 185, 187, 188, 189 top, 189 bottom, 193 top, 193 bottom, 194 top left, 194 top right, 195 top, 196-197

Maurizio Cargnelli and Duccio Zennaro
pages: 29 beans pictures, 39 bottom, 45, 46, 60, 62-63, 63, 76, 77, 78, 79, 80, 82, 84, 88, 91, 94, 95 top, 96 top, 96 bottom, 97 top, 97 bottom, 198

Stefano Carofei
pages: 200, 202, 204, 206

Giuseppe Ghedina
page: 64

Anna Illy Junior
pages: 103 top, 123

Elisabetta Illy
pages: 6-7, 16-17, 30, 100, 106, 107, 108, 109, 110, 112, 112-113, 114, 115 top, 115 bottom, 116, 117 top, 117 bottom, 118, 119, 120, 121, 122

Andrej Vodopivec
pages: 27, 32, 33 left, 39 left top, 40, 43, 47, 56, 67, 68, 124, 126, 128-129, 130, 132-133, 136, 137 bottom, 138, 139 top, 140-141, 144 top, 145, 146 top, 147, 148-149, 151 bottom, 154 top, 154 bottom, 155, 156 top, 174, 175, 176-177, 178, 179, 180, 181 bottom, 182, 184 bottom, 186-187, 190 left, 190 right, 191, 192, 194 centre top, 194 bottom, 195 bottom

Archivio Corbis Images
pages: 14, 18, 19, 23, 24-25, 48, 51, 61, 87, 89

Archivio Giotto Enterprise (courtesy of Fabrizio Chicco)
pages: 10, 13, 20-21, 28, 33 right, 37, 38, 70, 72, 73, 93, 95 bottom, 99, 104-105, 160-161, 163 bottom, 165, 167 bottom, 168-169, 172 top, 172-173 bottom, 173 top, 208-209, 214-215

Archivio illycaffè (courtesy of Fabio Silizio)
pages: 52, 54-55, 58